MW01503708

The Minyanaires

By Peter G. Engelman

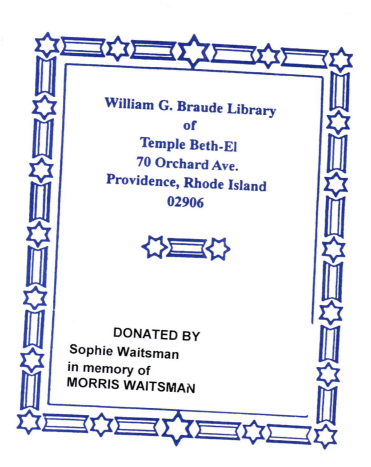

William G. Braude Library
of
Temple Beth-El
70 Orchard Ave.
Providence, Rhode Island
02906

DONATED BY
Sophie Waitsman
in memory of
MORRIS WAITSMAN

The Minyanaires

ISBN 0-9744277-0-5

Copyright © 2003 Peter G. Engelman

All Rights Reserved. No parts of this publication may be reproduced, stored in a retrieval system or transmitted in any form or by any means, electronic, mechanical, recording or otherwise, without the prior written permission of Peter G. Engelman.

Printed in the United States of America.

Additional copies of this book are available from the publisher.

Terumah Publishing
5 Pipe Hill Court, Unit C
Baltimore, Maryland 21209

Or visit our website:
www.terumah.com

Front Cover design and photograph by Peter G. Engelman
Back cover photograph by Judi Snyder

This book is dedicated to Minyanaires around the world, whose devotion and commitment to their faith provide the requisite minyan (quorum) for the Mourner's Kaddish.

Table of Contents

Foreword

One of the greatest *mitzvot* that synagogue Jews perform is to sustain a daily *minyan*. By doing so, they provide not only a place for other Jews to find comfort and spiritual fulfillment at times of personal angst and heartache, but they also create the truest feeling of a caring community. The fact is that the regular "Minyanaires" are the heart of every synagogue because they also serve to inspire others to take their Judaism more seriously and to sense the vital importance of every individual who helps to form a *minyan*.

Peter Engelman is symbolic of every Jew whose religious growth has been inspired by the daily *minyan*. His story is that of a person who, in seeking to honor his parents' memories, has given birth to his own spiritual biography. As a Rabbi, I am delighted to see that he has tried to articulate through an interview process the many varieties of the same impulse that drew him closer to his heritage. By doing so, he will have shown to others a path worth traveling when they are similarly challenged. Sometimes grief evokes hope and loss draws us nearer to renewal. May that be the result of his efforts.

Rabbi Mark G. Loeb
Beth El Congregation, Baltimore

Preface

On July 21, 2001, I lost my beloved mother, Doris, to complications of pneumonia and diabetes. I loved her dearly. Because of my mother's death, my daily routine for the past 24 months has changed dramatically.

I rise at 6:15 a.m., shower, dress, and drive to the Beth El Synagogue in Baltimore, where I attend daily *Shacharit* (morning) prayer services. I began attending morning services as a mourner following traditional Jewish law. Judaism requires that a mourner recite a daily memorial prayer called the *Kaddish*. For a child who has lost a parent, this prayer is recited every day for 11 months, beginning with the day of burial. For a parent, who has lost a child or one who has lost their spouse or sibling, the mourning period is 30 days.

Many modern Jews only observe the custom of saying *Kaddish* during the *shiva* (initial mourning) period and perhaps on the annual anniversary dates, when their synagogue sends them a reminder notice. It is easy to ascertain the reasons why secular Jews do only the minimum required of them; it doesn't require much exploration.

Most traditional Jews still follow the age-old custom and attend services for the full period of mourning. Once they complete their lamentation, many stop attending as they have met their religious responsibility. Some few mourners continue to attend daily services even after their mandated 11-month duty. These men and women are sometimes referred to affectionately with a colloquial term coined after the word "Millionaire." The "Minyanaires," are a special group who provide the *minyan* (required assembly of 10 Jewish persons) necessary for the continuing flow of mourners who, but for their presence, would not be able to recite the traditional *Kaddish* prayer. These distinguished people have an agenda that needs to be explored. This book is dedicated to them.

I first began to think about writing this book after completing my 11-month obligation. As I continued attending daily services beyond my religious requirement, I began to question my motives for continuing to show-up. Was it that I still felt the need for community prayer? Was it that I enjoyed my new early morning routine? Was it the social aspect of getting together with all of my new friends – discussing the news or just engaging in ordinary conversation? Maybe, it was the pride I felt when I was chosen to stand at the *bimah* (pulpit) to help lead the congregation in prayer. Perhaps, it was the humility I felt when I was called for a Torah *aliyah* (honor), where I read the prayers over the Torah and received a *Mi Shebeirach* (a personal blessing) from the Torah reader. Could it be the daily habit I acquired of putting on *tefillin* (phylacteries) that I hadn't worn since my Bar Mitzvah? Then again, perhaps it was the complimentary breakfast following the services. The poppy seed bagels with cream cheese, the hard-boiled eggs and coffee were certainly a drawing card for coming to *shul* – but then I could have indulged myself at home as well. Or did I find a new purpose in my life – a renewed reason for living?

After questioning myself extensively, I became aware that there wasn't a single reason for choosing to attend daily services. It was a combination of feelings and purpose that motivated me. There was something very comforting about the daily routine of praising God and seeking His blessings for my family and me. I had formed a new support system for myself without realizing it.

As I became aware of the answers for myself, I began to wonder if my reasons were the same as others who chose to attend the daily *minyan* service. I thought it might be interesting to explore with each individual member his or her reasons for attending regularly. The more I thought about it, the more intrigued I became. I enjoy writing and felt this would be an opportunity to write a story that was unique and unrevealed.

The nature of faith is a very individual and personal one. Most people don't speak about it – they just feel and practice it. Their reasons are often hidden within their hearts. Most people do not have the time or desire to query their sub-conscience or to analyze their feelings for doing what comes naturally to them.

I decided to approach this quest from the standpoint of a reporter. I would interview each of the approximately twenty regulars and record their responses. I would then present their thoughts in the form of narrative chapters.

These individuals literally keep our faith alive and flowing and their reasons for doing so are of utmost importance. Regardless of their motivation, the "Minyanaires" are to be publicly recognized for their contribution to the survival of Judaism. I hope this book helps to provide that recognition.

Acknowledgments

In writing a work like this, many people play a significant role in its completion. First are the Beth El "Minyanaires," without whom, this book would not have been possible. Their genuine interest and participation in the interviews and their willingness to share some of their personal history and most intimate feelings with the public is certainly an exceptional deed of kindness. It can be compared to a term in Hebrew, *Gemilus Chessed*, or the acronym *Gmach*, which means, a deed of kindness, especially an interest free loan. The "Minyanaires" shared their thoughts and words in this manner so that others may come to understand their motivations and devotion to their faith.

The participation of the Beth El Congregation's spiritual leaders in this endeavor embraces the anthology of lay opinions with their scholarly wisdom. It also makes this study a family affair, where all that form a part of the congregation are involved.

Then there are those who actually helped with the practical aspects of putting this book together. I thank Jeri L Ganz, an active "Minyanaire," for the many hours she spent proof reading and correcting this author's grammatical errors and for her many suggestions as to content. I also thank Stephanie Leikach of Beth El for her help with certain formatting and my wonderful wife, Sandy, for her many suggestions and encouragement.

I wish to credit Dianne Hales, contributing author, and *Parade Magazine* for permission to reprint excerpts from their article of March 23, 2003 entitled *Can Prayer Really Heal?* I also wish to pay homage to Beth El Congregation's former Rabbi Jacob Agus, of blessed memory, for his beautiful writings, excerpts of which are also contained herein.

Finally, I want to thank God for the inspiration He has given me to pursue this venture. As a learned sage once said, "God is wherever you want Him to be," and during the course of this work, He has been at my side encouraging me to move ahead and write a story that needed to be told.

Introduction

Beth El Congregation, as with other Jewish congregations across the nation and around the world, has daily *minyan* services for the benefit of its members and outside guests. The daily services of most congregations consist of three prayer sessions, namely *Shachrit* (morning), *Mincha* (afternoon) and *Maariv* (evening). Some smaller congregations, who have difficulty assembling the required quorum, may have only one evening service or in some cases only *Shabbat* (Sabbath) services.

At each of these services, members and guests recite a special prayer referred to as the *Kaddish*, to honor the memory of a family member or close friend who recently passed away. This special prayer is recited in various forms throughout the service. The origin of the *Kaddish* prayer is unknown. Its first use has been traced to the time of the second temple.

The Mourner's *Kaddish* is said standing, not only as a sign of respect to the memory of a loved one, but also, according to the sages, so that other members will notice them. In this way, the bereaved, by a show of identity, can receive the condolences of others in attendance.

The *Kaddish* is also recited on special holidays where memorial services are observed as well as the *Yahrzeit*, (Yiddish for anniversary) date of the death. The Mourner's *Kaddish*, like several other Hebrew prayers can only be recited when a *minyan* is present.

The *Kaddish* prayer does not specifically talk about death, but rather about the greatness of our God. We praise Him as the Creator of the universe and we ask that His Kingdom be established on earth during our lifetime. We bless and glorify His name and ask that there be peace on earth, in Israel and for us. The prayer is an affirmation of our faith in God in the face of our loss and bereavement.

The *shiva* period begins on the day of burial and lasts until the morning of the seventh day. The next period of mourning is known as *Shloshim*, Hebrew for the number thirty, because it lasts until the 30th day after burial. The final period of formal mourning is referred to as *Avelut* (Lamenting period) and is only observed by a child who has lost their parent. This period lasts for 12 months after burial. For 11 months of that period, the child of the deceased recites the Mourner's *Kaddish* every day.

It is believed that the soul of the deceased, including the most evil, requires 12 months to become purified before it enters the Kingdom of God. To make a distinction from the souls of the most evil, the sages shortened this one-year period to 11 months for those "good" souls about to enter His Kingdom.

Chapter One
Immanence and Immortality

As human beings, we are all aware of our mortality. No one escapes it. An old adage says, "there are only two things in life that are certain: death and taxes." The certainty of taxes is perhaps even more so than death, for with taxes, at least we know the due date. The date of our ultimate demise is and will always be elusive; still, we know one day it will come and, for most of us, that time is feared.

All of humanity yearns for some form of immortality. We wish to be remembered by those we leave behind. We search for a way to leave our mark once we are gone. In this regard, we make provisions to leave our personal and other worldly possessions to our family and friends, hoping that these reminders of our existence will help in some way to immortalize our souls or to stimulate in our loved ones the memory of our being.

Many of the affluent establish foundations and trusts in their name or make large contributions associating their name with hospitals, synagogues and other institutions where their name is prominently displayed. Very often, people or their families commission artists to sculpt or paint their likeness either in stone or on canvas in an attempt to achieve some type of perpetuity.

As rational human beings we realize, of course, that these mementos will not replace our physical being but we also reason that we have few alternatives. Those with more money and/or power may leave behind memorials of a more grandiose nature. In the end, the size or extent of items left behind will not return them from the grave or provide any greater solace to those left behind. Still, we refer to photographs, letters, tapes and other physical memorabilia of the deceased, in an attempt to keep our loved one's spirit alive.

In any discussion of death and immortality, the subjects of God, the soul and prayer are often intertwined. For many, prayer is a way to rationally communicate with the souls of loved ones that have gone to their eternal resting-place. When we pray to or for those who passed on, we invoke the name of God since we believe that their souls are in His safekeeping. In these situations, God becomes our messenger. We view Him as being inextricably linked to the souls of our departed.

Structured Judaic prayer is generally viewed as having three components, namely: affirmation, petition and contrition. Affirmation is the acknowledgement and acceptance of God, including various pledges of loyalty. Petition is that part of prayer where we ask God for his favor and blessings. Contrition, the third component, is the acknowledgment of sin combined with promises of atonement or repentance.

Prayer is an integral part of faith in that it is the communication vehicle between our Creator and us. Without it, faith quickly erodes. If one portrays God as our Creator without form or substance, without limits, and thereby beyond the comprehension of our limited conscience, it becomes natural to accept the idea or concept of prayer as the only way to communicate our thoughts to One that is so unknowable.

It is said that prayer soothes and refreshes the soul. It works to create peace and harmony within our bodies, similar to the effects of meditation, which has been likened to prayer. To seek peace and harmony within is a universal craving. Prayer is practiced by all religions of the world and is accepted universally as a means to achieving inner peace and serenity.

The March 23, 2003 edition of *Parade Magazine* included an article by contributing editor Dianne Hales entitled *Why Prayer Could Be Good Medicine*. In the article, Ms. Hales quotes varying scientific studies, which corroborate the healing power of prayer. In particular, one six-year study by Duke University found that the relative risk of dying was 46% lower for a group of 4,000 men and women, all over 64 years of age, who frequently attended religious services. Dr. Harold Koenig, director of Duke's Center for the Study of Religion/Spirituality and

Health, is quoted as saying of prayer: "it boosts morale, lowers agitation and enhances the ability to cope, in men, women, the elderly, the young, the healthy and the sick." Dr. Larry Dossey, a former internist who is the author of *Healing Words and Prayer is Good Medicine* and who prays for his patients daily says, "I decided that not using prayer on behalf of my patients was the equivalent of withholding a needed medication or surgical procedure."

Intercessory praying on behalf of others who might be ill is harder to prove scientifically, yet many studies have shown a significant benefit to this form of distant prayer. One study involving 2,774 patients, published in the *Annals of Internal Medicine*, found a positive effect in 57% and concluded that the evidence thus far merits further study.

According to the article in *Parade*, various polls taken of Americans found that 90% say they pray while 80% believe prayers can heal. Duke's Dr. Koenig states in the article, that he personally believes God heals people in supernatural ways, but he also says: "I don't think science can shape a study to prove it." He goes on to say: "we now know enough, based on solid research, to say that prayer, much like exercise and diet, has a connection with better health."

The Daily Prayer Book of Beth El Congregation (Copyright 1993), includes a passage of writings of the Congregation's beloved first Rabbi, Dr. Jacob Agus, of blessed memory, entitled *Reflections on Prayer: Function of Prayer in the Life of Modern Man*. On page 210, Rabbi Agus states:

> Essentially, our capacity for prayer is developed in the course of our growth in spiritual maturity. But the growth of our spirit does not proceed evenly in all directions at once. The attitudes of humility and dependence which the naïve and unsophisticated take for granted are recaptured only with difficulty by those who have tasted of the Tree of Knowledge. Proud of our inventive powers and scientific achievements, many of us find it hard to realize, down deep in our souls, that we are not complete unto ourselves; the true focus of our being lies outside ourselves; that to be at one with ourselves, we must relate ourselves wholly and deeply to the enduring reality around us. Modern depth- psychology has taught us to appreciate the abiding human need to

achieve "relatedness" and "at homeness" in the universe. In our sacred literature, this need is described as the universal yearning of all creation, of all living things as well as of inanimate objects, driven on the fundamental forces in the cosmos. "All that have breath in their nostrils" sing songs of praise to the Almighty, but in the non-human domain, it is always the same song, without conscience motivation or individual variation.

Man alone is capable of thinking of himself as an individual, set over against the universe. As we grow day by day in self-consciousness and self understanding, we become more deeply aware both of our loneliness and relatedness to the overarching all-inclusive Almighty God. As we strive for personal fulfillment, we realize ever more keenly the inexorable boundaries of our existence and infinite power and vastness of the Life of the Universe, which throbs but for a brief moment in our veins. Thus, as we seek our own deepest self, we come to find it ultimately in God. As Hillel put it, 'If I am not for myself, who will be for me? – But if I am only for myself, what am I?'

Chapter Two
My Story

I was born in 1940 in London, England. My parents were Czech refugees who fled from Hitler immediately after their marriage in March 1939. Their interesting story is the subject of another book.

My first recollection of religion is attending *chedar* (Hebrew for school) as a child of six. I remember the *shul* on North Avenue, where I attended classes. Its Principal and Administrative Director, Kopel Weinstein, headed up Har Zion Congregation. At the time, I attended secular school at P.S. 62, located at North and Smallwood Streets. After school, I remember walking over to Har Zion two or three days a week to attend Hebrew classes. I don't remember too much from those days since I was only six years old. I do remember bringing home various colored cards with Hebrew letters that I referred to as my *Ba Boh Beh* cards. Each week I would get another colored card with another Hebrew letter. I also recall making and playing with a cardboard *dreidel* (spinning top) on Chanukah.

When we moved from Baker Street to Cylburn Avenue, I was seven years old. My parents enrolled me at the Petach Tikvah Hebrew School on Denmore Avenue. I remember learning to read Hebrew for the first time and receiving my first *Siddur* (Hebrew prayer book), which by the way I still have, as a memento of my childhood. I recall getting awards and certificates for being one of the best readers in my class. It was at Petach Tikvah where I remember attending *shul* (synagogue) for the first time.

When I was around 10 or 11, my parents joined Chizuk Amuno Congregation. I switched Hebrew schools for the third time and attended their school on Chauncey Place. Hyman Saye was the Principal and I remember seeing his office on more occasions than I'd like to admit. At Chizuk Amuno, I took more classes in Hebrew studies and, ultimately, my Bar Mitzvah lessons with the noted Chazan (Cantor) Adolf Weisgall. My Bar Mitzvah was held on February 21, 1953. My Torah *parsha* (weekly Torah reading), Terumah, was from the book of Exodus and speaks of the Tabernacle and how it was to be constructed. This year marks the 50th anniversary of that special event in my life.

After my Bar Mitzvah, my exposure to religion was quite limited. I quit Hebrew school along with most of my friends and spent my spare time playing ball and getting into trouble. When I did go to *shul*, my only reason for attending was to meet girls. We used to congregate outside of the synagogue conversing with each other – at least until my father came out and literally pulled me inside.

Attending synagogue during my teens was done with great reluctance and only for the benefit of my parents. Except for Rosh Hashanah (the Jewish New Year), Yom Kippur (the Day of Atonement) and an occasional Bar or Bat Mitzvah, I hardly ever attended services. The same could also be said for my friends, who were always busy playing ball or going to social parties. When I entered the ninth grade at Forest Park High School, I joined the B'nai B'rith Youth organization known as "AZA," primarily for the social functions and to be a part of the in-crowd. As one can discern, my devotion to Judaism during my teenage years was at best tentative.

When I married and became a father, religion took on a new meaning to me. I remember having a *Brith Milah* (circumcision) ceremony for my two boys and a Hebrew baby naming for my daughter. As soon as they reached the entrance age, I enrolled them into Hebrew school. I took them to synagogue on the high holy days and tried to pass on the traditions I learned at home. We lit the Chanukah *menorah* (candelabrum), sang *Moaz Tsur*, (Rock of Ages) a German folk song, considered to be the most popular Chanukah song, and dressed them in costumes for the holiday of Purim (Festival of Lots). Celebrating the holidays with my children enhanced the traditional meaning of these occasions, but it was the ethical teachings of Judaism that seemed to impress me the most. I never acknowledged the ethics as God given, but reasoned that they were good guidelines for daily living regardless of how they were conceived.

For most of my life, the concept of God was vague and elusive. On those times when I attended *shul* and offered up my prayers to the Almighty, I often left the synagogue feeling spiritually unfulfilled. If God existed, you wouldn't know it by me.

When I was little, I remember my brother and I folding our hands in prayer and reciting the *Shema (E-l Melech Ne'eman)* (Hebrew prayer) at our bedtime. I recall the comfort of the ritual. As I grew older and into my teens, I abandoned the prayer as infantile and began to question the whole idea of God. For many years, I thought myself an agnostic. Webster loosely defines the term as "one who believes that the existence of a God is unknown and is probably unknowable."

Although I had sincere doubts about the existence of God, I was also at a loss to explain the many miracles of nature and creation I saw around me. When I was 14, my father bought me an astronomical telescope. I remember the awe I felt peering into that vast dark space filled with stars, planets, moons, rings and galaxies. I had more questions than answers, but still didn't think too much about God and his relationship to all of that cosmic beauty and wonder.

When my father died at the early age of 62 from a sudden heart-attack, I was 36 years old and didn't know what to do with my feelings of loss. My father was the most influential person in my life. I loved and admired him more than could be imagined. When he died, a part of me also died. To show my respect, I insisted that our family sit *shiva* for my father for seven days as required by traditional Jewish law; and as the eldest son, I tried as best I could to fill my father's shoes.

In this time of crisis, I turned to God to help me with my grieving. I mourned my father for the full 11 months attending at least one daily *minyan* service. I remember attending a *Mincha* (afternoon) service at the Social Security Building in Woodlawn as well as similar services conducted downtown, where I worked. I felt a degree of comfort going to the daily services. It was consoling to be with others who were going through the same type of bereavement. During those 11 months, I felt drawn to attend these daily *minyan* services almost to the point of compulsion. I felt I owed my father that respect – I felt it was the least that I could do to honor his memory.

Within a few months of my father's death, I divorced. Between the loss of my father and the stress of dissolving my marriage, my relationship with God became very crucial. My daily attendance at shul surely helped me through those terrible times.

In 1986, my faith in God was tested again. My eldest son became ill with Hodgkin's disease at the age of 19. The following twelve-month period was a very perilous time – a time that was wrought with uncertainty and fear. Through it all, I never blamed or abandoned God. Instead, I affirmed my belief in His goodness and hoped that He would carry me through this crisis. He did, as my son recovered from his illness but only for a short time. Seven years after his remission, my son was again struck down, this time with coronary heart disease. He required quadruple by-pass surgery at the early age of 27. Again, my faith in God was tested and my prayers answered. My son recovered from his surgery and has been fine ever since. I offer my thanks to God everyday for the healing power He sent our way.

On Saturday, July 21, 2001, my beloved mother, Doris, passed away at the age of 83. My mother was ill from a previous stroke suffered 14 months before her death. When Mom first became ill, she remained in a coma for about a week. Her doctor approached my brother and me and told us that it didn't look good for her – that it was probably a matter of a few days before she would pass away. I told the doctor my mother was a fighter and he shouldn't give up on her. I remember praying to God at that time. I prayed not only for my mother's recovery, but also for personal strength. I knew that if I could hold myself together, I could help my mother recover.

When Mom opened her eyes just a few days later, all the doctors were surprised. My brother and I were elated. We knew that she was on the road to recovery. I knew in my heart that God had somehow intervened. For someone who at one time considered himself an agnostic, this was an enormous admission. I rallied round my mother's bedside and summoned every specialist in the hospital. They came from all sides – neurologists, urologists, cardiologists, physiatrists, dermatologists, infectious disease and internal medicine specialists. I wanted my mother well and I used every resource I could think of to aid her in her recovery. Everyday, I looked to God for strength and everyday I felt renewed.

When my mom left the hospital, I knew that it was only through the Grace of God and the healing power that He passed unto me, that my mom was alive. Although my mother was not happy with her diminished condition, our family was delighted. We had our "Nanu" back and for us that was all that mattered.

When Mom died of pneumonia fourteen months later, she had given up. She was tired and ready to return to her Creator. Realistically, no amount of prayer would have sustained her at this point. When she passed away, we all knew it was at her choosing and upon her terms.

On the morning of her death, my brother and I, and our respective wives, visited with her at the hospital. At the time of our visit, Mom was comatose. None of us realized when we left her room how close she was to death. When we left the hospital, my wife and I drove to Towson to do some shopping. We were in the Museum Store looking around when I felt a funny feeling in my stomach. I instinctively left the store and called my mother's hospital room. As the phone rang, my anxiety grew more intense. When my mother's aide answered the phone, she recognized my voice immediately. Her voice broke as she told me that my mother was hardly breathing. Then, she told me Mom was taking her last breath. I can't explain how I knew to call at the very moment of her death, but I thought it oddly coincidental.

We left the shopping mall immediately and headed over to the hospital. When we walked into my mother's room, her aide was crying. Mom was still and at peace. It took us about 15 minutes to get across the beltway and over to the hospital. I felt my mother's forehead and it was still warm with fever. As I looked at her still body, I felt her spirit hovering over us. It was an unbelievable sensation – one that I never felt before and one I will never forget. There is no question that the spirit that I felt in the room was the soul of my beloved mother. Experiencing my mother's demise strengthened my belief in the hereafter and the existence of the soul.

After sitting *shiva* for my mom, I began attending the daily *minyan* at Beth El. Morning services start at 8:00 a.m. and I had to reorganize my daily schedule to arrive on time. My first 30 days of mourning were not easy ones. It was difficult trying to come to terms with the fact that my mother was no longer around physically. Gradually, through the help of others who were also in mourning and the support of the "Minyanaires," I began the process of healing.

It was in my first month of saying *Kaddish* that I met Jory Newman. Jory lost his mother a few weeks before I did. We happened to sit next to each other during services and it wasn't long before we became friends. Jory is twelve years my junior and, at first, our conversations were limited to the weather and non-personal subjects, but as we came to know each other better, we began sharing more personal things.

Morning and evening *minyan* services are conducted in part by the lay members of the congregation. Who conducts the service on any given day depends on who is in attendance and who is willing and capable of doing so. At some point during the first six months of our attending services, Jory and I were asked to lead the service together. Jory chanted the Hebrew and I read the English. Stan Berlin, who is in charge of the morning *minyan*, called on the two of us often. Doing the service with Jory was a delight for me and I looked forward to the honor whenever we were chosen.

During the ensuing months and now years, Jory learned the Torah and *Hallel* service, as well as *Maariv* (evening) and *Shabbat* services. He also learned some of the high-holiday readings and has demonstrated his competence from the pulpit on many occasions.

In the interim, I struggled to learn the morning services in Hebrew. After months of practice and perseverance, and with the words and melodies coming out of my ears, I sucked it in and volunteered to lead the *Shacharit* service in Hebrew. This experience, although nerve-racking, was one of the proudest moments of my life. Never did I ever imagine that, at the age of 63, I would be able to learn to read and sing the liturgy of my ancestors well enough to lead my congregation in prayer.

The day I led the services in Hebrew was a special occasion for me, to be sure, but it was also one of regret, for Jory and I would no longer lead the services together. Learning to chant the Hebrew cost me my job, so to speak, as I would now be called upon primarily to read the Hebrew portions of the service and with a different partner.

The evolvement of my friendship with Jory is no different than those of others who regularly attend services. Over the course of my two years of attendance, I spent many mornings observing the behavior of the other men and women in attendance. The camaraderie between them is easily noticed. There is no assigned seating in the chapel, yet members seem to always sit in the same seat next to the same person, day in and day out. If someone is out, the void is noticeable. The empty seat is immediately recognizable and there seems to be an air of concern until someone explains the reason for the absence.

It is said that human beings are creatures of habit. Inside the sanctuary, the situation is no different than on the outside. People arrive at services within a minute or so of their usual schedule – some early and some late, but always at the same time. Other than the dress and conversation, the routine among the participants remains the same. One would think that this sameness would be boring, yet for those who have made this observance their lifestyle, it is anything but.

It seems that the more I get involved, the more meaningful services become and, the more I look forward to attending. In the past, getting out of bed early in the morning was one of the most difficult tasks for me. Yet today, rising at 6:15 a.m. to attend services, has never been easier.

My story of faith is only one of many. As you read the chapters that follow, you will glance into the lives of some very spiritual people – lay people and clergy, each with their own panorama of experiences. Interviewing and writing about them and their beliefs has been a true learning experience and I thank all who participated in this endeavor.

This book is all about faith and commitment. I hope that reading it will enlighten you and make you think more about moving closer to God. The "Minyanaires" for whatever their reason, have chosen to make a daily contribution to the survival of Judaism. Their attendance at services and providing the needed *minyan* for mourners is a selfless act that helps to sustain those who are in need of healing. May God bless all those who have chosen this lifestyle of giving and may He cause His Countenance to shine down upon them.

Chapter Three
Stanley B. Berlin

Stanley B. Berlin has been honored and written about many times during his 31-year affiliation with Beth El. He is an exceptional man, who has devoted three decades of service to the congregation. His activities are only outdone by the energy this octogenarian exudes. Besides running the daily *minyan*, Stanley helps out with the congregation's newsletter and other mailings, is a *Shabbat* usher, a past and present officer of Club 50 (presently called Beth El Seniors), past co-chairman of the religious services committee, a member of the Board of Trustees, coordinator of annual blood drives, and a trusted mentor to many members of the synagogue.

Much has been written about Stanley's accomplishments including his war record, when he served our country in the Army Air Corps as a B-17 bomber pilot in missions over France and Germany. The proud father of twin daughters, Stanley became a widower at age 40, when his two daughters were only ten years old. Marrying for the second time in 1961, he enjoyed 36 years of married life before being widowed a second time in 1997.

With all of Stanley's devotion to Beth El, I was interested in his religious views. I asked him about his religious background and his beliefs. "In the beginning," Stanley says, "I attended *shul* three times a year. We belonged to Shaarei Zion in the 3500 block of Park Heights Avenue. All the services were in Hebrew and no English was spoken. I really couldn't get interested. My home was not very religious. My mother started to keep a kosher home because of her in-laws who were very religious, but when they never came around, she abandoned it."

I asked Stanley about his faith while he was serving our country. It seemed a natural question because of the daily risks he endured during his 25 bombing runs. I was surprised by his answer. "When I was in the Air Corps, religion didn't mean anything to me. I never prayed or thought about God at the time. I just tried to do my job and stay alive." He went on to say: "I had a lot of close calls and I was one of the few who made it, but God never entered into it, at least not consciously." Stanley considers himself a very pragmatic individual. He believes that we have complete control over our lives and that what we do with it is entirely up to us. He doesn't believe in any divine plan, nor does he believe in the soul.

Stanley's mother, of blessed memory, passed away in 1951 and it was then when he and his brother, Homer, came to *shul* to recite *Kaddish*, that he first put on *tefillin*. Stanley's in-laws were members of Chizuk Amuno and he and his family joined because of their affiliation. In the meantime, Stanley's father joined Beth El around 1949 and was one of the earliest members. Stanley's daughters were Bat Mitzvahed at Chizuk Amuno. Stanley's father, of blessed memory, died in 1972, and it was then that he became affiliated with Beth El. Although a member of Beth El, he recited *Kaddish* for his father at Beth Jacob as they had an earlier morning service that allowed Stan and his brother to be at work before 9:00 a.m.

When he first joined Beth El, Stanley was only mildly active. As time passed, he started to take on more responsibilities, becoming active with the Men's Club. "At times," he recalls, "we had 175 men attending the Sunday morning services and breakfast." Stanley took charge of the *davening* (prayer) schedule, appointing members who could lead the services in prayer.

Since his affiliation with Beth El, Stan has become much more religious. He says that 90% of his time at synagogue is religious and 10% is social. Despite all of his devotion to the *shul*, he still has slight doubts. He wonders why God permits so much suffering and inhumanity. He still asks why his first wife, of blessed memory, was taken from him at such an early age and why the Holocaust was allowed to happen. In this respect he says, "I guess you could call me a doubter." He doesn't believe in miracles and thinks that anything that appears that way is coincidental.

As a child, Stanley attended Isaac Davidson Hebrew School. He says, "we were taught how to read Hebrew and learned about all of the holidays, but they never taught us about faith and why we should believe."

Stanley enjoys educating himself. He attends many of the adult education classes given at Beth El and is a student of learning. I asked him if his faith was strengthened by his continuous education. He said, "no, but I enjoy the experience of learning."

Stan puts on *tefillin* daily. He says that it helps make him feel more connected to God. He wonders why others who attend on a regular basis don't do the same. It is apparent when talking to Stan that he is a deep thinker. He ponders difficult questions about God, as have Jewish scholars of old. I told Stan how much I admire him. He has become a mentor to me and to others and many regularly seek his advice and counsel.

Chapter Four
Nachman "Nat" L. Schein

Nachman "Nat" Lewis Schein was born in Austria in 1913. He came to New York in 1920 with his mother, grandfather, brother and two aunts. His father, who was a Rabbi, was already in New York. Nat is a Kohen (priest) by birth. As such, he can only accept the first or the last *aliyah* (Torah honor) and he is permitted to bless the congregation from the pulpit, which he says he has done on many occasions.

Nat attended the Yeshiva in New York and graduated in 1927 at the age of 14. Although Nat's father was a Rabbi, he served as a *Shamus* (Sexton) because he was unable to find a congregation. Nat thought of following in his father's footsteps, but became disenchanted after coming to the synagogue one day and seeing his father on his hands and knees scrubbing the floor.

Nat had a beautiful tenor voice and loved to sing. He auditioned for Paul Whiteman and was accepted to sing with his orchestra. Later, he went to Cleveland and took a job with a radio station as an announcer. From there, he went to Columbus and then to Providence RI, where he sang as part of a trio.

Nat tells the story of how he once went to the racetrack and bet on a horse with the name of his girlfriend. He won $17,000. A week later, he says, "I was broke." When I asked him what happened to the money, he replied "riotous living." While in Providence, he received a job offer from the SEC. At the time, he was making $300-400 a week singing, but accepted the job as a clerk with the SEC for only $21 a week. After a year, he left and went to work for the Social Security Administration, where he worked as a file clerk, then a proofreader and finally an editor. Nat left Social Security to work for the NLRB (National Labor Relations Board) in D.C., where he helped draft legislation. When the war came, Nat served in the Army Transportation Corp. After the war, he worked in a liquor store and then for the Schenley Company, where he served as the D.C. State Manager. He moved to Baltimore in 1951 to take a position with Schenley. Nat met his wife, Rose, in Baltimore and married at age 40. The couple will celebrate their 50th anniversary this May.

Although Nat considers himself Orthodox, he enjoys coming to Beth El, a Conservative synagogue. He says, "it doesn't matter where you attend services...you are Jewish." Nat has a strong belief in God and absolutely believes God hears our prayers; that He is everywhere and hears everything. But when I asked him about prayer specifically, he says, "I don't believe that much in prayer. I still pray, but sometimes you don't know why you do things."

Nat talks about how, in his thirties, he stopped attending services for about ten years. When I asked why, he replied he didn't know. I asked him if he had lost his faith during that time. He said, "No, I just took a hiatus. I can't even remember why."

I asked Nat whether he believes in a soul. He said he believes in a soul and an afterlife, but as to where the soul goes when you die, he says, "I don't know, but it goes somewhere." Nat attends Sabbath services at Beth T'filoh Congregation. He says "I love to hear the Chazan (Cantor) chant the *Shemoneh Esrei*. (The 18 blessings, also known as the *Amidah*). He says, "it is like a concert."

When I asked him about attending morning services at Beth El, Nat said he enjoys the fellowship there. He talks about how nice the fellows are. He points to the last time he was ill and how he received house and telephone calls. He says, "I'll never forget that."

Nat has been attending regular *minyan* services at Beth El for about ten years. He says, "I used to greet the mourners until I couldn't walk. I'm usually the first one here and it's hard for me to get up and greet them." He relates how he once came to services and there were only nine people present. He was the tenth person and, without him, the mourners would not have been able to recite the *Kaddish* prayer. He says, "I felt so exhilarated knowing that I made a difference."

Nat taught a Yiddish course at Baltimore Hebrew University for many years. He enjoys being with people and interacting with the members. It is a pleasure knowing Nat and listening to his story and his views on Judaism.

Chapter Five
Jerome Rudich

I interviewed Jerome on Monday, March 17, 2003. Jerome has been attending daily *minyan* services at Beth El since his wife's passing in July 2002. According to Jewish law, a spouse is required to recite the *Kaddish* prayer for 30 days. Jerome has been reciting it for nine months at the time of this writing. I asked him why.

Jerome replied that he was married for sixty years when his wife passed away. He first met her when she was 12 years old. The couple married when he was 19 and she 18. He knew her practically all of his life and they shared a lifetime together. He says, "I feel closer to her when I attend services. I feel like I am honoring her memory." Jerome talks about his wife in the most endearing terms. "She was always involved in charity from the first time I met her. Even when I knew her as a child, she was always raising money for different causes," he said. "She was an organizer, a leader and was always participating in different charitable causes."

Jerome grew up in an Orthodox home. He attended *chedar* at a synagogue on Glen Avenue and Park Heights. "Everything was in Hebrew," he says. "There was hardly any English spoken." While attending, he wore the traditional *Tallit Katan* (undergarment with fringes) with the *tzitzit* hanging out from under his shirt. He said that all activities were performed in groups. He said that he felt very religious at that time because of the atmosphere. As he got older and into more secular crowds, he stopped wearing the *Tallit Katan* and began to move away from the Orthodox ways. Jerome's mother always kept a kosher home and was the more Orthodox of his parents.

I asked Jerome of his concept of God. He replied that he never thought about it much. He says, "I believed in it because it was taught to me." He believes in the soul, but says he's not sure where his soul will go after he dies.

Jerome believes that God hears our prayers, but says, "it is hard to know if He intercedes." He describes God as a cloud above us that knows everything we are doing. He doesn't pray much outside of *shul*, but feels like He hears him, particularly when he addresses the picture of his wife. Although Jerome has friends and a son and daughter who are supportive of him, he says, "I am very much alone."

I asked Jerome if he was helped by any of the regulars who attend the daily *minyan*. He said that when he first came, he knew only Eddie Offit. Now, since coming every day, he has come to know more of the regulars. He doesn't remember anyone in particular greeting him, but he says that he has become friendly with many of the other mourners. He enjoys the chanting of the prayers and likes the fact that the transliteration is printed next to many of them. Although he grew up in an Orthodox environment, he has forgotten a lot over the years and would like to be able to read the prayers more fluently.

Jerome stated that he never witnessed what he would call a miracle. He says that to him a miracle is when someone who is deathly ill make a miraculous recovery. Jerome questions why God permits people to suffer before they die. He says, "that is one thing I've never been able to figure out."

Chapter Six
Betty H. Zlotowitz

Betty H. Zlotowitz is an outgoing and vivacious woman, who is heavily involved in Synagogue and community affairs, including many fund raising activities. Betty, who is 75 years old and proud of it, was raised in an Orthodox family, who practiced all of the traditional customs of our faith including the laws of *Kashruth* (keeping kosher).

As a child, she attended Hebrew school and was Bat Mitzvahed at the Shaarei Tfiloh Congregation, located on Auchentoroly Terrace and Holmes Avenue. Betty enjoyed her Hebrew education and, after her Bat Mitzvah, she was eager to continue; however she was discouraged from going further because it wasn't considered appropriate at that time for a girl to study Talmud. That didn't stop Betty, however, for she continued to sit in on the men's discussion groups where they discussed Rashi (biblical commentator of the middle ages) and the *Gemorrah* (part of the Talmud). She remembers being the only girl at the group and that the men were glad to have her around.

Betty met her husband, Al, of blessed memory, when she was 13 years old at her Bat Mitzvah reception, which was held at her home. Her first date with him was a year later, when she was 14. They were married five years later, when Betty was 19. Betty and Al were married 49 years. They had a son and two daughters, all of whom are very close to her.

Betty started attending the daily *minyan* services seven years ago after the untimely passing of her husband. She says about the Beth El "Minyanaires." "They were the friendliest group of strangers I had ever met and they have been an enormous source of strength and support." Since coming to the daily services, she has become involved in all sorts of projects at the Synagogue, including the Social Action Committee, of which she is chairperson, the Beth El Seniors, where she served as President, and the Beth El Board of Directors. Betty is to be installed shortly as Vice President of the Beth El Seniors. She believes strongly in the power of prayer. Betty believes that God not only hears her prayers, but answers them as well. She believes that the soul is an individual quality, but that the spirit of that soul is passed down from generation to generation.

Betty reads Hebrew fluently and understands much of what she reads. Receiving an *aliyah* is, according to her, one of the highest privileges one can have. She recalls the first time she was called to the Torah and how strange she felt. With her prior affiliations in the Orthodox tradition, women were not allowed to read from the Torah. She says, "I have gotten used to it and I love to participate." She believes that if one is offered an *aliyah*, it should never be turned down.

I asked Betty if she greets the new mourners who come to the synagogue to say *Kaddish*. Her response to me was "not normally, unless I know the people. I think it's the proper thing to do and I don't know why I don't do it; now that you mentioned it, I will have to consider doing it more often."

I noticed that on Wednesday mornings some of the women do not attend the morning service. I asked Betty why she doesn't come on Wednesdays. Her answer was not surprising. "I don't know, to tell you the truth," she said. "I know that some of the other women don't come on Wednesdays either and so I just do the same."

I asked about miracles and whether Betty ever witnessed one. Betty hesitated and then said she believes that, although she never witnessed it, the birth of a baby was a miracle. She also said that nature is full of miracles. She talked about the trees and the glaciers of the Northwest Passage, all of which seemed to impress her very much as examples of a miracle.

Betty looks forward to remaining active in the synagogue for many years to come. As one who has come to know her well, I know her determination will go far in helping her achieve her goal.

Chapter Seven
Stanley Silverman

Stanley came from an Orthodox family. His family attended Agudas Achim Congregation, located in the 4200 block of Park Heights Avenue across the street from the old Avalon Theatre. His father, of blessed memory, was a founder of the congregation. He has two older brothers and two children.

Stanley began attending services regularly at age 15, after losing his father, who passed away in 1951 at the early age of 53. Stanley recalls how hard it was losing his father at such a young age. He was just entering high school and it was a difficult adjustment for both him and his mother. Attending services was of great comfort to him.

He began attending Beth El about 20 years ago, after his uncle's family joined the congregation. He recalls that, at one time, his family was so large they occupied two rows of seats in the Offit Auditorium.

Stanley particularly enjoyed listening to Cantor Hammerman chant the prayers. He remembers bringing his wife to the synagogue before they were married so that she could hear the Cantor perform songs from *Fiddler on the Roof*. He says, "I felt like I had just been to a Broadway show."

Stanley contends that he is in communication with God 24 hours a day. He says, "I feel comfortable that He is on my side and that He helps me to achieve my daily goals." His main concern is good health and the health of the people around him. He makes personal *Mi Shebeirach* (direct prayers of healing) prayers to God everyday for people he knows are ill. He uses both their English and Hebrew names.

Stanley admits he comes to *shul* for selfish reasons. He says, "the moment I come into the building, I enjoy myself. I have developed strong friendships with the other fellows. Every day or two, they call me or I call them, plus the service itself; it's all connected." When he receives an *aliyah*, he considers it a great honor and an honor for his parents as well, because their names are recalled.

Stanley greets all of the new mourners by introducing himself and then introducing them after the service. He says, "once I hear their name, I remember them from then on. I remember meeting Morty Nettler when he first came here from New York. He didn't know anyone and we became friends and I introduced him to everybody."

I asked Stanley if he had any further comments. He told me he thought what I was doing was a wonderful thing. He reminded me that Rabbi Loeb discussed the motivation of the "Minyanaires" in one of his sermons and that this interview reminded him of that sermon.

Chapter Eight
Morton Nettler

Morty Nettler is an unassuming guy who loves attending services for the sheer enjoyment. Having grown up in the Bronx, Mort came from an Orthodox family that practiced traditional Judaism. During World War II, Mort served in the Air Corp as a parachute rigger. He served 38 months in the service and came out with the rank of sergeant. Mort has three children, two of which are twins. He moved to Baltimore in 1985 because two of his children lived here. A year later, in 1986, he lost his father, of blessed memory. He began attending services at that time in order to say *Kaddish* for his father.

Since his first days of saying *Kaddish*, Mort has been a regular attendee at the morning *minyan* services. The year 2003 marks his 17th anniversary as a member of the Beth El "Minyanaires."

Morty believes that God is our soul and that He guides us in our daily living. He believes that we are all his creation and that everything in life is *beshert* (predestined). He believes that we have control over our lives by God's intention of allowing us to make our own decisions; however, that is also controlled by fate. Mort defines a good life as being kind to others and not meddling in other people's lives.

Mort first wore *tefillin* when he was Bar Mitzvahed and continued until he entered the military service. He attends *Shabbat* services regularly and has been an usher for many years. He enjoys handing out *Siddurs* (prayer books) to the congregants as they enter the synagogue on *Shabbat* and the high holy days. He feels that volunteering gives him an incentive for living and a purpose in life. He enjoys the Beth El services and the camaraderie that it provides him. Morty says, "I was never very religious, but I have strong beliefs." I asked him whether, during his lifetime, he ever lost his faith. "I never had it to lose," he said laughing.

I asked if he ever witnessed a miracle. Mort's answer: "I don't think so; things that have to happen, happen. From the time we are born, we are slated to die and it's all according to how we live our life."

Mort doesn't like to conduct services or make announcements in front of people. He says, "I just sit there and do my own thing." He is saddened by the fact that many of the men he used to see at services have passed away.

Chapter Nine
Gilbert Kramer

Gil Kramer grew up in Northwest Baltimore. As a young man he attended the Lubavitch Ari Shul on Quantico Avenue off Old Pimlico Road. The *shul*, which was led by Rabbi Herschel Liebowitz, of blessed memory, later merged into Ner Tamid, currently located off Greenspring Avenue. His mother kept a kosher home, changed the dishes for Passover, and observed most of the traditions of Judaism. Gil went to Isaac Davidson Hebrew School on Shirley Avenue and was Bar Mitzvahed there. After his Bar Mitzvah, he quit Hebrew school, but continued to attend *Shabbat* services.

I asked Gil about his belief in God. He is quite ambivalent about his beliefs. He says, "there could be someone up there who is a lot smarter than we are, but I couldn't say what form." He doesn't believe that God is any type of being as such. He says, "my beliefs have changed over the last ten or fifteen years. I believe differently than I did 30 or 40 years ago. I don't know if there is a God in heaven and I feel most people believe in God because they fear death. I don't know if there is a heaven or a hell. I believe when you die, you die, that it's a long sleep." He believes that death is a part of life.

I questioned Gil about prayer. "I don't know if there's a God that hears our prayers," he said. "I say prayers, but I don't know if there is anyone listening." I asked Gil about his belief in a soul. He said that if there were souls they probably wouldn't come into effect until after you die, but again reiterated that he didn't know whether he believes in it.

Gils says he attends services because it something to do and he likes it. He says, "I feel relaxed and they are a nice group of people to meet and talk with." He has attended the morning services for about two years, although he has been coming to Beth El for some 15 years. When I asked what prompted him to begin coming two years ago, he surprised me with his answer. I thought, like most people, he started attending as a mourner. "Actually," he said, "I started attending after I moved my office to my home. I got up early and didn't have anything to do in the morning, so I decided to come to services."

Gil told me he didn't consider himself a religious person by nature. He says, "no one has ever died and come back to tell me that there is a God." As far as the literature, he says, "it's been written by men and handed down from generation to generation and there is no way to tell if it's true or not." Regarding the 10 commandments, he said he believes in them and they make sense. He added, however, that he is troubled with events occurring two or three thousand years ago.

Gil feels everyone has a right to believe in whatever they want and he wants to believe in whatever he believes without having a hassle from anyone else. He recites *Kaddish* four or fives times a year for different people and believes the morning services are important for Judaism to continue. "Whether you believe or you don't believe, it's still a *mitzvah* (commandment)(good deed) to come to services," he says. "It gives continuity to our children for the future."

Chapter Ten
Jory L. Newman

Jory L. Newman is one of my closest friends at Beth El. We met almost two years ago after the untimely passing of our mothers, of blessed memory. For 11 months, we sat next to each other, rising every day to recite the Mourner's *Kaddish*. Two years later, we still sit next to each other and share the news of the day.

Jory grew up in Northwest Baltimore on Cadillac and Rogers Avenues. He was raised in a Conservative home, and his family attended Chizuk Amuno Congregation on Stevenson Road. His mother kept a kosher home and his parents observed all of the traditions of a Jewish home. Going to services on Friday evenings was a usual practice at the Newman home and Jory enjoyed the rich melodies that were chanted by the then Chazan, Adolf Weisgall, of blessed memory. Jory attended Hebrew and confirmation classes at Chizuk Amuno and celebrated his Bar Mitzvah there as well.

When he obtained his driver's license, his social life took precedence over his attendance at *shul*, however he continued to observe many of the traditions of the holidays. He particularly enjoyed the Passover Seders at home with his family. After graduating high school, he attended the University of Miami and graduated with a Bachelor of Arts degree in Sociology.

Jory always felt a strong connection to Judaism. "I have always been very proud of my religion," he says. "It was something that I always felt." Although his attendance at services was sporadic during his earlier years, he says, "I never lost my faith."

He believes that there is a connection between prayer and feeling in communication with God. He describes placing himself in that special spiritual setting while saying certain prayers, like the *Amidah*, the silent devotion that all congregants recite as part of the morning prayers. He prays outside of synagogue as well, but feels there is a special spiritual energy that takes place when a community of Jews prays together.

Jory studied and mastered the morning and evening services to the point that he regularly leads the *minyan* in Hebrew prayer. He has a beautiful tenor voice and chants the melodies with a stunning resonance that seems to be enjoyed by all. Jory considers his achievements in synagogue to be an honor and privilege. He says, "It's been a delight in my life, more than I can even verbalize."

I asked him if he believed in the soul. Jory said he believes, as a Jew, if you believe in God, you have to also believe in a soul. He points to the *Amidah* prayers, where we recall the memories of those who passed on before us. As to the human soul, referred to in Hebrew as *n'shama*, he says, "If there were no *n'shama*, there would be nothing to remember them by." He says that how a person affected you while they were living is the manner in which you remember them, and not necessarily by their human form.

Asked about reincarnation, Jory stated, "I think it is an interesting concept, but I am not prepared to go that far." He believes that naming a baby after someone who has passed away immortalizes his or her soul.

He gets a great deal of satisfaction from doing things for others. He is an active participant and volunteer. He greets the new mourners and takes them under his wing.

Jory sees miracles in everyday life. He describes the bud on a tree, a flower, or a beautiful sky as examples. He hesitates and then talks about the smiles on the faces of his grandchildren as the biggest miracle. He says, "It's a tough world out there and we become immune to the daily wonders.

Chapter Eleven
Lewis Penn

Lew Penn has been a member of Beth El Congregation for almost 40 years. He is married with three grown children. Lew came from an Orthodox family and as a child, he attended Agudas Achim Shul located in the lower Park Heights area. When he was 11 years old, he went to services at Beth Yehuda Congregation, which at the time was under the direction of Rabbi Perlmutter. He also attended Isaac Davidson Hebrew School for a number of years before becoming Bar Mitzvahed at Agudas Achim. He married in 1947 and attended Beth Jacob for a number of years before coming to Beth El around 1963. His younger son and daughter were Bar and Bat Mitzvahed from the pulpit of Beth El. Lew grew up around Cold Spring and Reisterstown Roads, not far from Park Lane.

Lew started attending the morning *minyan* after his mother, of blessed memory, passed away in 1998. Lew was very close with his mother, always making daily telephone calls. Lew recalls the support he received from the "Minyanaires." "It was very comforting to have friends that understood what I was going through," he said.

Lew is a deeply religious man, who prays daily. When he lost his sister, of blessed memory, he says he was drawn closer to God. Lew is a positive thinker. He always looks on the bright side. He says, "you have to remember the good things rather than the bad." When it comes to people, he feels similarly. "I try to think that everybody has a good side and I look for that good side. I never met anyone that I hated," he says. "I believe that there is a lot of evil in the world, but as far as my relationships, I have never come across anyone like that."

Lew believes that God gives us strength. He talks about some of the reverses in his life and how things always managed to turn around. He says, "not all things turn out 100%, but I have done the best that I could to overcome these [bad] things."

I asked Lew why he continues to come to services, long after his obligations to his mother and father have passed. He responded, saying, "I continue to come to services because I need the feeling of being close to God. I enjoy the entire service," he says.

He greets new mourners, looking out for those wearing black ribbons. As far as miracles, he has some feeling that they do exist. He points to his father who, in 1961, was diagnosed with an aneurysm of the brain. The doctors had literally written him off and Lew and his family were called out of town to his bedside. At the time, Mr. Penn was only 54 years old. As it turned out, he recovered and lived another 40 years, passing away in 2001 at the age of 94.

Lew says he is not sure about whether life is predestined. "I don't think we have any control over these things. I believe in fate. I think you have to be in the right place at the right time. Certain things happen and you ask yourself why, but you have to keep going."

Chapter Twelve
Edward J. Offit

I interviewed Edward J. Offit on Thursday, March 13, 2003. At 97, Eddie is one of the last living members of the original founders of Beth El Congregation. The initial meeting for the formation of the Synagogue was held at the home of Eddie Offit's brother, Maurice, in 1950.

Eddie was born in 1906. As a child he lived with his parents and grandfather, who were Orthodox and pious Jews. Eddie spoke only Yiddish as a young boy. He first learned to speak English in the first grade of secular school. According to Eddie, he was speaking fluent English by the end of his first year in elementary school. He had seven years of Hebrew school and was Bar Mitzvahed from the Bikur Cholim Synagogue on North High Street in East Baltimore. Eddie and his family were in the shirt manufacturing business for many years under the name of Aetna Shirts.

I asked Eddie about 17 questions relating to his faith in God and his reasons for attending daily services. Here are the questions and answers.

Q. "Do you believe in God?"
A. "Yes, I believe in God...I am strong believer in God."
Q. "Do you believe that God hears our prayers?"
A. "I believe He hears everything."

Q. "Do you believe it necessary to be in *shul* for God to hear our prayers?"

A. "No."

Q. "Have you ever questioned the existence of God?"

A. "Many times things happen, like when a young child dies and you ask where's God."

Q. "How did you get your faith back?"

A. "I am a great believer in God."

Q. "Do you believe God has a master plan?"

A. "It's all part of life…I don't know about any plan. I can't answer that."

Q. "Do you believe in the soul?"

A. "Everyone has a soul…everyone has a conscience. I think the soul is the brain."

Q. "Do you believe the soul goes up to Heaven when you die?"

A. "I think that's a fantasy, I don't believe that."

Q. "Do you believe that some people are born with a good soul and others with a bad one?"

A. "Whether someone has a good or bad soul is a conversation; everyone's mind functions differently."

Q. "How long have you been attending daily *minyan* services?"

A. "I started attending Beth El services in 1950 when it was formed."

Q. "How many daily services do you attend?"

A. "I only attend morning services because I don't drive at night. If I could drive at night, I would attend every night."

Q. "Do you attend Sabbath services?"

A. "Yes, I enjoy it very much…I enjoy the sermon, the Cantor…everything."

Q. "What part of the daily *minyan* services do you enjoy the most?"

A. "Meeting the fellows and the daily conversations. I enjoy listening to what everybody has to say; you learn something every day."

Q. "Do you greet new mourners, when they come to say *Kaddish*?"

A. "I always greet mourners. I met Jerry Cohen and Stanley Fradin that way, when they lost their loved ones. I made friends with them and I enjoy their company."

Q. "Do you consider coming to *shul* your duty or obligation?"

A. "No, I love to come to *shul*. I feel very comfortable. I come to pray and I enjoy the morale...the company I am with."

Q. "Have you ever lost your faith?"

A. "Sure! Sometimes you ask whether there is a Lord."

Q. "Have you ever witnessed a miracle?"

A. "I don't think so...never gave it any consideration. I can't answer that, never gave it much consideration."

Q. "Do you have anything you would like to add?"

A. "There are a lot of changes that have been made in the *shul*, some that I don't like. The *shul* is successful, so it's hard to say whether it's good or bad."

Chapter Thirteen
Jeri L. Ganz

Jeri is a single mother with two lovely daughters. She was raised in a Conservative Jewish home in Rockville, Maryland by parents and grandparents who were very active in the Jewish community. Jeri is the eldest of four children. Jeri's grandfather, Daniel Ezrin, of blessed memory, was very active at Adas Israel in Washington, D.C., where Jeri's family has belonged since 1940. Jeri was very close with her grandparents. There were fourteen grandchildren in the family and Jeri says that she shared a special bond with her grandfather. He used to take her to Beth El on Saturdays during the years he worked there and she looked forward to those times when they would spend quality time together.

As a teen, Jeri was very active in USY (United Synagogue Youth) and she made many friends there, some of which have lasted through the years. She went to Hebrew school at Adas Israel in D.C. and had her Bat Mitzvah and Confirmation there. After being Confirmed, Jeri went to Israel for six weeks with her Confirmation class on a Ramah program.

Jeri attended Brandeis University where she majored in American history and minored in legal studies. While at Brandeis, she also took courses in French and Hebrew. When she completed her studies, she was fluent in both languages. After graduation, she took a trip to

France and Israel and was able to communicate well in both countries. Jeri continued her education at the University of Maryland Law School in downtown Baltimore. She graduated with a law degree and today is actively engaged in practicing law with a local corporation.

Jeri's grandfather, Daniel Ezrin, of blessed memory, passed away in 1976, just two weeks before her Bat Mitzvah. He was supposed to do the Torah reading on her special day and Jeri still questions why God took him away from her at that time. Before he passed away, Daniel was actively involved at Beth El as the congregation's Ritual Director. He tutored the B'nai Mitzvah students and read the Torah at *Shabbat* morning services.

Jeri joined Beth El in 1989 and has become an active participant in the synagogue. Both of her daughters, Dani and Rachel, attend Hebrew school. Jeri is very involved with them in *Project Mishpacha*, a special family learning program created by the joint efforts of the congregation's Senior Rabbi, Mark G. Loeb, and Education Director, Dr. Eyal Bor. Jeri notes that Hebrew school studies are different today. "When I went to Hebrew school, I learned everything by rote." Today, especially with this particular program, children are taught to understand the why's and wherefore's of Judaism and they get a chance to practice it as well through their participation in services at the synagogue and their religious reinforcement at home.

Jeri began attending the morning *minyan* after her grandmother, of blessed memory, passed away last October. Jeri's grandmother was such an important part of her life that she began attending the *minyan* to honor her memory. Although she had no obligation to say *Kaddish* for her grandmother since her parents are still alive, Jeri felt it important to do so. She comes almost every day and says, "participating in the *minyan* helps to center me." She continues, saying, "having two active children and working full time [is difficult]; it's a great way to start your day and I have made some very good friends at the *minyan*." She explains that when she misses a day, she feels her day is not complete. For her daughters, Beth El has become like a second home and they both feel very comfortable around the "Minyanaires." When they are able to attend, both Dani and Rachel participate in the services, helping to dress the Torah with their mother when she receives the honor.

Jeri feels very strongly about Judaism and leading a Jewish life, but continues to struggle with the concept of an all-knowing, loving and caring God, who allows bad things to happen to his people. She mentioned she would like to take classes on the subject so that she can get to some of the answers that seem to bother her. She says that her doubts have not stopped her from living a Jewish life and her feelings about Judaism.

I asked Jeri about her feelings on the soul. She replied saying that she believes on a certain level that it exits and hopes that some of the attributes of the people who have passed on are there [in those still living]. As far as miracles, she points to the birth of her children, but admits that she hasn't given the question much thought.

I assured Jeri that many of her questions would be addressed in this book and that I am hopeful, as its author, that it would help to shed some light on a very complicated subject. It was my pleasure to interview Jeri who is not only a lovely person, but a wonderful mom as well.

Chapter Fourteen
Rene F. Daniel

Rene grew up in Manhattan in an area known as Washington Heights, comprised of mostly German Jewish immigrants. He and his older sister were raised in an Orthodox Jewish home where he observed the laws of *Kashruth* and attended services regularly at Emes Wozedek, led by Rabbi Max Koppel. He graduated Hebrew school and was Bar Mitzvahed in New York. Rene was married in New York and moved to Baltimore about 27 years ago, when his daughter was six and his son two. Rene originally came to Baltimore because of a business opportunity offered to him. He began to attend the morning *minyan* after his sister, of blessed memory, passed away some five and half years ago. About seven years his senior, Rene's sister was ultra Orthodox. She had six children and would, had she now lived, been a grandmother to over 40 grandchildren.

When she passed away, Rene decided to say *Kaddish* for her for the full eleven months. He felt that this was the respectful way of honoring her memory and her devout way of life.

Rene's concept of God is that of a spirit of being that oversees all of the operations on earth. He is aware of everything that goes on and has a master plan for all of us. Rene believes that God has complete control of our lives and that we don't possess the power to alter his plan. Rene works out four days a week but he says, "I do it for myself, because I enjoy it. I don't think it will change anything concerning my longevity. Life is a one way ticket. When you're time is up, it's up," he says with a smile. "My 92-year old mother has a saying. She says, 'life is a'comin and a'goin,' and I think she is right."

Rene is a firm believer in prayer and believes that God listens. He especially believes in saying the prayer known as *Refuah Shleima* or *Ro-fei Cholim*, which is the eighth blessing of the *Amidah* prayers, wherein we ask God to heal someone who is ill. He says he feels deeply connected [to God] during that particular prayer and thinks a lot about the person for whom he is praying.

As far as religious training, Rene believes that the Hebrew schools should do more with teaching children about understanding what they are reading. He says, "I learned everything by repetition and did not understand a word." He doesn't think memorization is the way to instill true values. He repeats that he could *daven* fluently in Hebrew, but didn't understand a word he was saying. Today, Rene still *davens* the same but reads the English translation as well.

Regarding the attending of daily services, Rene says, "I love it! It starts my day off right." He enjoys the camaraderie. "These guys are a wonderful bunch of people," he says. "They are the glue that holds everything together. Most of them are older than me and retired but they still enjoy hearing about my workday."

As concerns new mourners, Rene says that he tries to greet all of them, but knows that in the beginning it is difficult for them. He tries to get them to assimilate by inviting them to join the breakfast that usually follows the service.

I asked him about his belief in miracles and his answer was: "I think children are miracles...when you see in a child the heart and life of someone else – that's a miracle."

Chapter Fifteen
Gerald E. Cohen

Jerry Cohen grew up in the lower Park Heights Avenue area of Baltimore and attended Hebrew school at Isaac Davidson. He was Bar Mitzvahed on April 25, 1942 from Lubavitch Nusach Ari Congregation, a small congregation on Quantico Avenue. After his Bar Mitzvah, he attended Agudas Achim Synagogue under the direction of Rabbi Shapiro. He was a charter member of the Akiva Boys, a religious group formed by Rabbi Shapiro. His mother kept a kosher home and he has always observed all of the Jewish holidays. As a young boy, he attended a summer session of the Yeshiva in Brooklyn, New York.

Jerry, who is married to his wife Arlyn for 52 years, has two grown children and one grandchild. His son and 16-year-old grandson live in Hawaii and his daughter lives in Baltimore. He is an affable 74-year-old man who makes friends easily and looks twenty years younger than his actual age.

In 1954, Jerry was drafted into the Army. After basic training, he served with the 101st Airborne Division for eight months in Ft. Jackson, S.C. and was then deployed to Frankfort, Germany, where he served for 15 months, beginning with the 4th Infantry Division and then with the Army V Corps. When he was deployed to Germany by ship, he served as acting Jewish Chaplain onboard the "U.S.S. General Rose," a troop ship that carried close to 3,000 soldiers. Once in Germany, he served as acting Chaplain at the Frankfurt Jewish Chapel, whenever the regular Jewish Chaplain was away on assignment.

He began attending services at Beth El after his father, of blessed memory, passed away in 1980. He sat next to Eddie Offit at that time and has been sitting next to him ever since. When he leads the congregation from the *bimah*, Jerry is at his best, having memorized the entire service. He says he learned the entire service by heart after his first year of saying *Kaddish* for his father. Although he keeps his *Siddur* in front of him and turns the pages as he *davens*, Jerry keeps his eyes shut as he recites the prayers from memory. One wonders why he even bothers turning the pages.

Jerry describes coming to services as his way of starting out his day in the right direction. He says, "coming to services provides the most spiritual uplifting moments in my life. I feel much better in the morning when I leave than when I come in." He talks about the camaraderie after the *davening* as helping to make his day. "Just to sit down at the table [with my friends] makes the whole day worthwhile." He says jokingly that if he wasn't picked on, he couldn't go to his office in good spirits.

As far as his beliefs, Jerry thinks that "God is the number one guy, and has the power over all of us." He sees Him as a spiritual being who has a divine plan for all of us, but believes that we have control over our lives. He thinks that our death is predestined, but believes that we can make our lives more enjoyable by exercising and eating the right foods. He recalls that his mother lived to be 98 and, until the last three weeks of her life, was in excellent health.

Regarding prayer, Jerry is a firm believer in it. He says, "I believe that God is listening and that He has an effect on the way we lead our daily lives. I pray every morning for those who are sick. I have been praying for one person who has been very sick for some 12 years – she is still around, so it must be working." He believes that prayer is not only good for healing another, but is also healthy for the person doing the praying.

Jerry says he believes in miracles and describes them as something that happens unexpectedly. He mentions his mother's longevity as an example.

When I asked him for any last comments, he said, "I look forward to everything I do in *shul*, whether it is praying in my seat or praying from the *bimah*, and especially the camaraderie that has developed over the years."

Chapter Sixteen
Stanford J. Schneider

Stan Schneider grew up in East Baltimore, living on Collington Avenue between Monument and McElderry Streets. Stan's father, of blessed memory, passed away at the early age of 29 from complications of appendicitis. At the time, Stan was only five years old and was raised by his widowed mother with help of an aunt and uncle. As a child, he attended *chedar* at Baltimore Talmud Torah on Broadway. He attended services at Beth Hamidrash HaGadol Shul under the leadership of Rabbi Vitzick.

After moving from East Baltimore to Coldspring Lane, Stan and his wife, Sylvia, attended services at the Petach Tikvah Shul on Denmore Avenue in Northwest Baltimore. Cantor Hillel Lipsicus and Rabbi Axelman officiated at the time. Stan and his family came to Beth El Congregation some 40 years ago to enroll their six-year-old daughter in the congregation's Hebrew school. Stan and his wife have been active in the synagogue ever since.

Stanford is a deeply religious person who believes in God and prayer. He believes God to be what you want Him to be. "I often talk to God," he says. "I realize there are a few other people in the world besides myself and most have more problems than I have, but I feel you need to keep in touch with Him." Stan and his wife lost their son to AIDS when he was only 32 years old, and both certainly would have good reason for questioning their faith, but just the opposite is true. Stan and his wife were empowered by their son's early demise and turned their tragedy into a living memorial for their son, performing volunteer work at the Hopkins Hospital AIDS floor where they offer comfort and support to many of those who suffer alone from this dread disease. Stan says, "no one should die alone," and he is determined to make a difference in the lives of these unfortunate victims.

Stan says he often feels God's presence. He prays while he walks and believes God hears his prayers. He believes that all have a soul to keep us on an even keel. As far as an afterlife, Stan laughs saying, "I can't prove or disprove it, since I have never met anyone who has been there, but I think there is something there."

Stan started saying *Kaddish* for his uncle, of blessed memory, when he passed away some 30 years ago. He has continued to come to morning services ever since. He stands and recites the *Kaddish* every day, although he hasn't suffered a family loss in many years. He says, "maybe it's wrong for me to recite the *Kaddish*, but I feel there is someone in this world that is deserving of having the *Kaddish* recited and so I continue to do it."

Stan served our country for two years in the Army during the Korean War and was stationed in Frankfort, Germany. While in the service, he sought out synagogues and attended services there.

He believes God has a divine plan over which we have no control. He mentions the process of natural selection and believes this is God's way of controlling our population.

Stan loves coming to services and the camaraderie that he has come to enjoy. He warns that, if you plan to miss a service, you had better tell someone or you can expect a call from one of the other members within a day or two. He believes Beth El has a special group of "Minyanaires" and he is glad that they are being recognized for their contribution over the years.

Chapter Seventeen
Alvin Book

Alvin Book began attending the daily *minyan* 15 years ago after the passing of his sister, of blessed memory. As he approaches his 80th birthday, Alvin recalls his youth and has a clear recollection of past events.

As a child, he lived in East Baltimore on Chester and Baltimore Streets and was raised in an Orthodox household. His grandparents raised both he and his sister since his mother worked full time. He attended P.S. 27 Elementary School, P.S. 40 Junior High and Patterson High School.

He recalls attending *shul* with his grandfather, of blessed memory, at Bais Hamidrash HaGodol, located on Central Avenue near Orleans Street. His Hebrew education began with a man named Bennett who, although not a Rabbi, knew as much as one. After his Bar Mitzvah, Alvin attended Talmud Torah but says, "I didn't learn much there."

Alvin helped his grandparents in their grocery store until he was about 15, when they all moved to Woodbrook Avenue in Northwest Baltimore. After graduating high school, Alvin worked for the Glen L. Martin Company, where he was employed for a year before being drafted into the army. Alvin served in the infantry and landed on Omaha Beach at Normandy on June 12, 1944, six days after "D" day. He was wounded after the battle of St. Lo during the great push towards central Europe. For his heroism, he was awarded the Purple Heart, the Bronze Star and the Combat Infantry Badge.

After the war, Alvin married the former Rosalie Posner in 1948. The couple has two children and two grandchildren and will celebrate their 55th anniversary this fall.

Insofar as his religious beliefs, Alvin says, " I have always believed in God." He recalls reciting the *Shema* often during his time in combat. During the heat of battle, Alvin said he prayed constantly and felt God's presence all around him.

"I believe that God is within all of us," he says. He likens God to a spirit and believes he hears all of our prayers. When things work out, he credits God as the reason; when they don't, he believes God has His reasons as well. "I think there are reasons we don't know about, but even then I believe in God."

Alvin believes that the soul and God are synonymous, but that each has individuality. He says, "God has freedom to think and has given us that same freedom." He also believes that if we are righteous, we will have a good life. When things don't work out, he thinks that God has his reasons and prays that things will work out.

Alvin's regular attendance and participation at Beth El has not gone unnoticed. Several years ago, he was honored by the Beth El Brotherhood and was written up in the congregation's Bulletin. Besides leading services for the daily *minyan*, Alvin has been active in synagogue activities for many years.

"I love to come to *shul*," he says with a broad smile. "When I put on my *tefillin*, I feel a closeness to God. I love the camaraderie and feel like we are all one big family."

Alvin believes that reciting the *Shema* is the most important part of the service. He compares it to saying the *Pledge of Allegiance*. He would like to see all the Bar and Bat Mitzvah candidates recite it from the *bimah* as part of the *tefillin* ceremony. As for greeting mourners, he says, "I always greet everyone, especially when I see someone wearing a black ribbon."

I asked Alvin if he ever witnessed a miracle. His answer was no surprise. "I have witnessed a lot of them," he said. "When I was in Normandy, I was stationed next to a narrow road and heard the noise of a tank coming towards me. It was a Nazi tank and when they saw me, they opened fire with both machine gun and artillery rounds. I was leaning against the sand with my face and body buried into the embankment. A shell penetrated the sand and exploded with yellow and green smoke but I was not hurt. The tank rode right past me thinking that I was dead. I was saying *Shema Yisroel* as loud as I could. Another miracle occurred when our own airforce bombed us. Over 200 men in our regiment were injured and some 20 were killed. My foxhole caved in and I had to dig myself out. The next day a P47 plane strafed us and dropped a 500-pound bomb that landed only two feet away from me. It didn't go off. It was a dud. Those were miracles."

Eventually, Alvin's luck ran out and, on July 25, 1944 he was wounded, but thank-God not severely. He spent two months in the hospital recuperating from his wounds before returning to his infantry unit.

As an interesting side note, Alvin related to me a story about the Purple Heart on his license plates. When the Department of Motor Vehicles began issuing plates with the Purple Heart on them, he felt funny applying for them. Alvin is a modest man and he didn't want to appear that he was somehow showing off. What changed his mind was a comment by a Congressman, who said something about Jews not fighting in the war. The comment raised Alvin's ire and it was then that he ordered the plates. Alvin quoted the *Mishna* saying "when you do something good, you should share it with your family. I consider everyone at *shul* to be my brother and sister and I am proud to be here and to be a part of it."

Chapter Eighteen
Stanley B. Fradin

Stan Fradin has been coming to Beth El morning services regularly since the passing of his beloved wife two years ago. He was born into an Orthodox family and his mother kept a kosher home. He attended parochial school at The Talmudical Academy through the second grade and then transferred to public school for the rest of his secular education. He spent about four years at Har Zion's Hebrew school on North Avenue until the age of 10 and then completed the rest of his studies at Beth Tfiloh Congregation, from where he was Bar Mitzvahed.

I asked Stan what he learned in Hebrew school. He replied that his education was very basic, learning about the holidays and how to read Hebrew, but not much in the way of learning about God and our faith. I went through my customary questions with him, asking first about his belief in God. Stan said, "I always believed that there was some force out there, whether you call it God or some kind of ectoplasm. I believe that He hears our prayers and that He does intercede in our lives." He says that he believes in divine intervention and to a certain extent in fate.

"When my wife passed away, my faith was shaken," he says. "It wasn't so much that I doubted the existence of God, but rather why He did this to me." He is heartened by the fact that he believes his wife is in a good place and that he can communicate with her. He points to an event where he asked for a sign within a week after her passing and received it. Whether it was coincidence or had some other rational explanation is not important to him. The fact that it happened is enough. Stan is not sure about the soul. He says, "I haven't thought about it a lot. I do believe in an afterlife, but how it takes place, I don't know."

I asked Stan why he continues to attend services long after saying *Kaddish* for his wife. He said, "I believe when you take something out, you should put something back. The *minyan* served a great need that I had at the time. It provided me with great comfort and belonging and helped me to get over the grief." He talks about the friends he has made and how he looks forward to the daily conversations. He says, "I will continue to come to services as long as they will have me or until something else stops me from coming." He explains that this is something he wants to do rather than something he feels he has to do. We spoke about the concept of miracles. Stan's reaction was typical of his strong faith. He said, "I believe that there are happenings, but I don't believe I have ever witnessed one."

Stan's face lights up when he talks about the "Minyanaires." "The Beth El morning group is a very homogenized one," he says. "New people meld in very quickly. If someone wishes you a *Yasher Koach*, (literally - may your strength be increased) for doing a good job with your *aliyah*, you don't have to worry about the sincerity…it is coming from the heart."

Chapter Nineteen
Harold E. Resnick

Harold was brought up in Rochester, New York by Orthodox parents who kept a kosher home. Harold attended *chedar* five days a week and Sunday school as well at Beth Joseph Congregation in Rochester. When he was about 14, after his Bar Mitzvah, Harold was offered a chance to go to the Yeshiva in New York, but he declined.

In 1946, Harold's father had a business opportunity presented to him in Los Angeles. The family moved to California and Harold completed his high school education there. After high school, he attended Los Angeles City College. During the course of his studies, he was drafted into the Army because of the Korean conflict. Harold trained in the Army Counter Intelligence School at Ft. Holabird, Maryland. During his service at Holabird, Rabbi Drazin, of blessed memory, of the old Shaarei Tefillah Congregation, used to bring a contingent of college girls from the University of Maryland to Ft. Holabird. He conducted Friday evening services with four or five of the Jewish soldiers stationed there. It was on one of those occasions that Harold met his wife, Gilda. When the army sent him to Salzburg, Austria, the two carried on a long distance relationship until Harold returned from the service and the two became engaged. They were married in 1953 and will celebrate their 50th wedding anniversary this coming November. Harold and his wife have two grown children and four grandchildren.

Harold started coming to Beth El after the death of his beloved parents, of blessed memory. He has been coming regularly for morning services for about eight years. Harold feels that coming to *shul* is a good way to start his day.

He believes in God and believes that He watches over everybody. He says, "I believe He may hear our prayers. I pray primarily inside the *shul* and outside when I say the *Yahrzeit* prayers for my parents." He relates that many of the important decisions he has made in his life have been directed by the Almighty. "I have never been in trouble, I have a wonderful wife and two good children, and He has blessed me with grandchildren."

As far as the soul, Harold believes that it [the soul] is how a person treats or feels about another person. "Does he do it with respect or humility; does he appreciate or understand that some people are not as blessed as he may be and treats them accordingly? You may be born with a soul, but I think for many people they don't realize it until they get older."

I asked Harold about miracles. He replied that the birth of his son and daughter were miracles. He also mentions the survivors of the Holocaust that he debriefed in the Displaced Persons Camp overseas. "These people lost their whole families and had no homes to go back to. The fact that they survived was a miracle."

Harold says that he has gained many wonderful friends coming to the morning *minyan*. He says of them "they are true friends and that the camaraderie is one of the main reasons that I look forward to coming to *shul*."

Chapter Twenty
Michael S. Dopkin

Michael Dopkin grew up on Bancroft Road in Northwest Baltimore. He started Hebrew school at the old Chizuk Amuno on Eutaw Place and followed them to their new building on Stevenson Road. In 1964, his family moved over to Beth El and it was there that he had his Bar Mitzvah. He remembers Meyer Rabinowitz, of blessed memory, teaching him his Bar Mitzvah lessons. Michael recalls that, after his family joined Beth El, he loved to attend adult *Shabbat* services with his father, of blessed memory, who passed away almost three years ago.

After a lapse of many years, when Michael was about 35, he became very interested in his Jewish identity and again began attending Saturday morning services on a regular basis. Once he started attending, his parents followed suit. He had cousins who were also members, so the family always sat and prayed together. Gradually, Michael became more active and started to chant Haftorah portions.

When his father, of blessed memory, passed away in August of 2000, Michael began coming to morning *minyan* services on a daily basis. He recited the *Kaddish* prayer for the full 11 months. Once he completed his obligation, he continued to attend the morning services on a reduced schedule. He chose Tuesdays and Fridays as his regular days, wanting to take advantage of the days that were convenient as well as when various members of the clergy attended.

Michael enjoys music and plays the piano for recreation. He delights in listening to classical music. He also participates in Cantor Thom King's adult choir. During his period of mourning for his father, Michael learned from Cantor King how to chant the daily morning service, after which he began leading services. He enjoys leading the morning *minyan* and continues to do so once or twice a week.

Michael shares the belief with many others who think that God is unknowable and that you can't assign human characteristics to Him. As far as prayer he says, "I believe prayer is for us – it provides something for us. Whether God hears it or not, I think there is a need for people to go outside themselves to a higher plane, that's not mundane and that transports us to a different level of consciousness." He goes on to say that, "even if there isn't a God, perhaps it's a good idea to act as if there were one, so as to enable us to realize that there are more important things than the everyday petty things that we are concerned about."

Michael enjoys being a part of the Beth El family. He points out how helpful it was to him to be a part of that family when he lost his father. He said that it was very comforting to him that Rabbi Loeb and Cantor King officiated at the funeral and at the *shiva* house. He said that knowing they knew him and his family meant a lot and offered him the consolation he needed at that difficult time. He went on to talk about how nice it was to be able to be with the morning *minyan* where many had experienced similar losses.

Michael is a big believer in saying *Kaddish* in a community rather than by himself. He says, "this is where religion really shines. Having the comfort of the clergy and the congregation really helps in time of loss." Michael is thankful for the full life of his father (he passed away at 83) and feels more appreciative about his life than mournful about his death.

Michael doesn't subscribe to the theory of predestination. He believes that we all have free will and he doesn't believe in the phrase "it was meant to be." He doesn't like the idea of attributing everything that happens to God and feels that there are more questions than answers when it comes to these matters.

Michael started putting on *tefillin* after his father passed away. He had an old set with frayed leather straps that he didn't feel comfortable wearing. He replaced them with a new pair after doing some interesting research on the types available. He says to lay *tefillin* is very important to him in that it is a custom that goes back over 2,500 years. He enjoys being linked to the generations before him that practiced the same *mitzvah*.

I asked Michael his feelings about miracles. His answer was similar to others of whom I asked the question. "I think watching my nieces grow up from birth is amazing," he says. He points to the accomplishments in the medical field and how his father was able to take advantage of these God inspired miracles of man. He believes that the inspiration that empowers people to perform such wonders may indeed come from a divine spark.

Michael recently lost his cat, Chelsea, after having her as his pet for 16 and one-half years. He says that losing her was almost as difficult as losing a family member. He has a hard time believing that Chelsea was without a soul and feels that anyone who has ever loved and been loved by a pet would agree. Chelsea was buried in the pet cemetery operated by the Humane Society of Baltimore County.

An active participant in the congregation, Michael is involved with the Beth El adult choir, and serves on the Religious Services Committee. He is currently involved in Project 613, where Beth El is having its own Torah being written by a sofer (scroll writer) in Israel. It will take another year or so before the Torah is completed and there are many activities planned around its creation and dedication.

Chapter Twenty-one
Kenneth Baum

Kenny Baum was born and raised in St. Louis, Missouri. His parents were Orthodox, *Shomar Shabbos* Jews, who kept a kosher home and attended *Shabbat* services regularly. He attended *chedar* at the early age of four, and was taught by two different Rabbis, the latter of which taught him how to *daven* and prepare for his Bar Mitzvah. He was Bar Mitzvahed at Beth Israel Congregation in St. Louis. He remembers that on that day, a *minyan* of ten men came to his house and walked him to the *shul*. In addition to reading the Maftir and Haftorah portions, Kenny had to also give a 45 minute speech, half of which was in Yiddish and the other half in English.

Kenny served in the U.S. Navy from 1948 through 1950 and the Army from 1952 through 1954. His term in the Navy was the result of his volunteering and his term in the Army was because of the draft. During the Korean crisis, he served at Aberdeen Proving Grounds in Maryland in a variety of positions and units.

In 1953, Kenny met his wife, the former Anita Schleider, at the Army base in Aberdeen. Volunteers from the Jewish Community Center brought Jewish women to the base to meet the Jewish soldiers stationed there. Kenny was married in April 1954, while still in the Army.

After his discharge, Anita's parents, who were in the kosher catering business, asked Kenny to work in their business. For eight years thereafter, he worked in the company's warehouse learning the business. After that period he was brought into management as vice president and served in that capacity for the next nine years.

With encouragement from his wife's family, Kenny opened the Knish Shop in February 1970 as an extension of their catering business. He operated the kosher food establishment for 28 years before selling it to his former partner. For the last five years, Kenny has been semi-retired, working three days a week for Seven-Mile Market, a Pikesville, Maryland kosher supermarket.

Kenny, who has been married for almost 50 years, has three children, and one grandchild. He is a happy go-lucky type of person, who counts his blessings everyday. He is a strong believer in God. He says, "God is the All Being; He is above everything in this world, He is our Creator and I pray to Him everyday." He believes that prayer can be recited anywhere and not necessarily just in the synagogue. He cannot prove that God hears his prayers but says, "I hope He hears me."

He believes in the soul and defines it as an inner being that will continue on when his body gives out. He thinks about the members of his family who have passed on and looks forward to the time when he will join them.

Kenny's father passed away at age 46. His mother passed on at age 83. When his father died, Kenny asked God why He took his father at such an early age. For a time he struggled with the question, until the answer came to him. Kenny reasoned that had his father lived longer, he would have spoiled his children because of his impending success in business. Because he died young, his children were forced to pull themselves up by their bootstraps making them more independent adults.

A fatalist at heart, Kenny believes that all things are *beshert*. He points to the way he came to Maryland and met his wife and the wonderful life that has sprung from that relationship.

Kenny comes to the morning *minyan* on a regular basis and has been doing so ever since his mother, of blessed memory, passed away some thirteen years ago. He says, "I enjoy coming, praying and being near to God and being with wonderful people." Kenny says that he recites the *Refua Schleima* prayer everyday for his family and those who are ill. He also prays for the children of Israel and for peace in the world.

As far as miracles, he talks about the miracle of birth and the blessings that have been bestowed on him. Kenny says he wakes up in the morning and looks around at all of his blessings. He says, "as long as my wife and family are all healthy and feeling well, I am happy – it's perfect; I love it!"

Chapter Twenty-two
Jillian R. Shure

For purposes of balance, I thought I would interview my 10-year-old granddaughter, Jillian, to see how her young thoughts differed from those of the older and wiser "Minyanaires." Aside from the fact that she is my granddaughter and I am slightly prejudiced, I was truly amazed at her answers to such deep questions. One would assume that a child of that age would not have the comprehension to understand and be able to express her thoughts so well.

Jillian lives in Olney, Maryland, a growing suburb of Rockville. She was born in Salt Lake City, Utah on October 15, 1992. She attends the Glen Elg Country School in Howard County, where she is presently in the fifth grade. She attends B'nai Shalom Hebrew School and their junior congregation services on *Shabbat*. She has been attending Hebrew classes for about four years and seems to enjoy learning all about her faith.

I asked Jillian about her belief in God and how she would describe him. She said, "I believe in God. I think He is a spirit who lives everywhere. I believe He lives inside of us too. I don't know why I believe that, but I do. Nobody can see God, so you can't prove that God is a spirit, but I believe He is because most Jewish people believe that God is everywhere and a living person can't be everywhere, so God must be a spirit."

When I asked her to go into more detail, she answered: "A spirit is like a personality or who you are. It's like a soul. A soul is like a spirit. You are made with a soul because your body protects the soul and the soul is who you are...your personality." I asked Jillian her opinion about what happens to the soul when a person passes away. "When a person dies, the soul lives on forever," she said. "The soul goes to Heaven. The person doesn't go there...only the soul."

In discussing prayer, my granddaughter said, "I believe that God helps you when you need Him, but most of the time, you make your own decisions without help from anybody. I believe in prayer and that God hears our prayers when we mean what we say; but if we just read the prayers and don't mean it, it doesn't mean anything to Him." She went on to say, "If you pray for something that is possible, then He might help you to make it come true, but if you pray for something that is almost impossible, like wishing for money, then He won't give it to you because He expects you to work for it."

I asked Jillian about her opinion on reincarnation. "I don't believe in reincarnation," she said, "because the world would be too crowded...people would die and just keep coming back." I continued my questioning by asking her thoughts about Heaven for good people and Hell for those who were bad. She replied. "I believe that all people go to Heaven because I don't think God would separate good and bad people." She said, "bad people have paid for being that way by going to jail or by not living a full life and why would God make them relive jail again in Hell?"

Jillian says, "I believe in miracles because without them, life would be very boring. A miracle is something that you never expect to happen that happens. I sort of experienced a miracle when I had to find a new school and at the last minute it happened. Another miracle was that I adapted so quickly to the new rules and made lots of friends."

Chapter Twenty-three
Sandra Winters – Ritual Director

Sandy Winters is the Ritual Director at Beth El Synagogue. Besides being responsible for organizing the daily *minyanim*, Sandy is also an active participant, often reading the Torah on Mondays and Thursdays, as well as on *Shabbat* and many of the Jewish holidays. As Ritual Director, she shares the responsibility for overseeing all of the B'nai Mitzvah teaching with the congregation's new Director, Art Wien, who joined the synagogue staff in 2002 and has taken over the individual teaching. Today, she is primarily involved in the adult B'nai Mitzvah classes, as well as teaching adult education classes.

Sandy grew up in a traditional family. Her parents were children of Eastern European immigrants. They kept a kosher home and the family attended services regularly. Sandy's parents joined Chizuk Amuno Congregation when she was a child. She attended Hebrew school and was confirmed there. Her favorite teacher was Mr. Jack Epstein. She continued her Hebrew studies at Baltimore Hebrew High School, a part of the Baltimore Hebrew College. Her secular education was completed at Forest Park High, not far from her home in the Ashburton section of Baltimore.

Sandy attended college at Boston University, where she graduated with a Bachelor of Arts degree in education. Her social life revolved around Jewish activities and, in 1959, she spent four months working on a kibbutz in Israel. Unbeknownst to her, her husband-to-be was also in Israel at the time, working on a kibbutz just 18 miles away.

They actually met at Columbia University, where Sandy got her master's degree in education.

After they married, Sandy and her husband, of blessed memory, joined Beth Israel Synagogue in Randallstown. Both she and her husband became involved in the activities of the Conservative *shul* and, in time, her husband became President of the Congregation.

Sandy studied languages in high school and college and became very proficient with them. She reads and speaks fluent French and Hebrew and has taught both. She was teaching French in public school when she had her first child. She became a stay-at-home mom until after her second child was born. When they were three and five, Sandy became involved in Jewish education, working part time for Beth Israel and then later at Beth T'filoh Day School. As she taught and studied, her reputation as a teacher of Hebrew studies gained her a reputation in the Jewish community.

When Rabbi Loeb learned of her adeptness, he made inquiry into bringing this talented scholar and teacher to Beth El. The congregation needed a Torah reader and someone to assist Rabbi Samuel Schwartz, of blessed memory, who at the time was the Congregation's Ritual Director. Sandy accepted the position of Assistant Ritual Director 11-years ago. When the Principal of the Hebrew School, Joseph Lipavsky, of blessed memory, suddenly passed away, Sandy took over teaching the Bar and Bat Mitzvah classes. When Rabbi Samuel Schwartz, of blessed memory, passed away several years later, Sandy assumed his former position of Ritual Director.

Sandy says, "I enjoy teaching adult education the most. Five years ago, I would have said working with the Bar and Bat Mitzvah classes, but today I am happy doing what I do." I asked Sandy how she compares the youngsters of today versus those of yesterday. "I think children today are very cynical of religion and don't take their education seriously," she said. "I believe TV and the media have had a negative effect. I also find that the divorce culture has had a very big influence on children. Being able to give children a strong Jewish identity is getting harder and harder because of the [changing] family environment."

When I asked Sandy about her belief and concepts of God, her answers were deep and philosophical. "I am a big follower of the writings of Harold Kushner, the author of *When Bad Things Happen to Good People*," she replied. "I believe that God is a very limited God; I don't believe in an all powerful God that can change the world. I believe that God was the Creator, but I don't believe in a personal God," she says with fervor and conviction. Sandy goes on to say that she believes the idea of God is what it is that we learn in terms of our Jewish values. She believes further that prayer is an expression of Jewish identity and she identifies strongly with that identity. Sandy says, "I recite the prayers because there is an esthetic value. The origin of the Hebrew word, *tefilah*, is self-examination; that to me is what prayer is [all about]. It pulls me into a structural thing because it's something that I wouldn't do otherwise."

As far as the soul is concerned, Sandy is somewhat ambivalent in that she hasn't spent much time thinking about it. She says that, to her, a soul is what makes people different from animals. It is the fact that we are able to think. She doesn't believe in a spiritual soul, but believes instead that we keep memories alive by reciting the *Kaddish* prayer and observing our loved one's *Yahrzeit*, which is observed annually, forever and ever. Sandy is very analytical in all of her beliefs. She is an avid reader and has studied the subject of religion from every angle. She doesn't consider herself "religious" in the normal context of the word, but sees herself as deeply identified with Jewish customs and traditions. When she teaches, she doesn't express her personal beliefs, but passes on the meaning of the text with which she is working. She thinks that everyone should form their own beliefs based on their own interpretations.

As far as the future of Judaism, Sandy believes it is headed in the right direction. "From my own experiences with the interest in adult education during the last ten years, I believe Judaism is in good shape." Sandy thinks we may not be able to get to the kids until they are in their 50's, but eventually she hopes they will become involved.

Having listened to Sandy's pragmatic answers, I hesitated to ask her about her belief in miracles. I truly believed the question would be answered with a resounding no! I was surprised to hear that she actually does believe in one and only one miracle, that being the miracle of birth. This seeming departure from Sandy's otherwise analytical approach to the questions on divinity stems from her personal experiences with the birth of her grandchild. Despite her otherwise rational responses, she is at a loss for words when it comes to explaining the mechanisms of the human body that miraculously harmonize into producing a living being.

Chapter Twenty-four
Rabbi Steven P. Schwartz

Rabbi Steven P. Schwartz was born in Chicago, lived in Baltimore until age five, and moved to Binghamton, New York where his father, a physician, took on a new position. He grew up in Binghamton, attending Hebrew school and services at a Reform congregation. He was Bar Mitzvahed in New York and led a traditional Jewish life, going to services on the holidays and always taking an interest in Jewish learning and customs.

Rabbi Schwartz's first thoughts of becoming a Rabbi occurred when he was only a youngster of about 10 or 11. As he grew into his teens and then went on to college, the thought of becoming a Rabbi became lost in the transition. He earned his degree in psychology at Brandeis University and received his Masters at the University of Maryland.

When he graduated from college, Rabbi Schwartz was hired by a State agency where he applied his psychology skills in helping people who were former State patients return to society, assisting them with a broad level of support, including job and independent living counseling. He worked with these patients for four years before turning his thoughts to the Rabbinate. He explains his motivation to change careers as being somewhat of a calling. When he was 24 or 25, he began taking classes in Hebrew and Judaic studies at Boston Hebrew College. He began to read many books on Jewish subjects and became increasingly aware of his Jewish identity. His first serious consideration of joining the Rabbinate came after a co-worker suggested the idea to him. It was hinted that here was an opportunity for him to combine his humanity skills with his newfound love for the study of Judaism. At the time, Rabbi Schwartz had recently married his wife Becky, whose father was a Rabbi and was a big influence in his decision to change careers. After many meetings with both his father-in-law and other mentors, he decided to apply to the Jewish Theological Seminary in New York, but was rejected on his first attempt because of his educational deficits in the field of Jewish study. The seminary encouraged him to attend the one-year Mechina program at the University of Judaism in Los Angeles, where he would receive the prerequisite courses for the Seminary.

After completing the one-year course in California, he applied to the Seminary again and was accepted. He continued his Rabbinical studies in Los Angeles for another year and then in Jerusalem for still another. He returned to New York, where he completed his studies at the Seminary. Rabbi Schwartz recalls the emotional moment when he was ordained at the Seminary. At a special morning program, each student is given a new Tallit, which is placed around him by the Dean of the Rabbinical School. At that precise moment, he is officially ordained as a Rabbi.

Rabbi Schwartz recalls that, when he married, it was the first time he ever kept kosher and had any kind of regular rhythm of the *Shabbat*. He came to love the practices and points out that much of his direction came from the atmosphere that he shared with his new family.

Rabbi Schwartz came to Beth El after a very involved selection process that included many interviews with many different congregations. He remembers it being a "crazy time" in his life where he was running from one state to another, meeting with committees and congregational members all of whom were interested in hiring a new Rabbi. He ultimately chose Beth El because of the reputation of Rabbi Marc Loeb, who was known as an excellent mentor for his assistants, and the fact that Beth El would provide his family with opportunities that were not available with smaller congregations.

I asked Rabbi Schwartz what was the most difficult part of becoming a Rabbi. He said, "the most difficult thing for me was learning Hebrew. I don't take easily to learning languages," he confided. He now admits that although he still has some trouble speaking the language, he now fully understands and can read it fluently.

I asked Rabbi Schwartz about his experiences here at Beth El and he responded saying, "It's been a fantastic experience…my biggest challenge is the long hours and not being able to be with my family as much as I would like." The Rabbi's schedule is sometimes at great odds with his responsibilities to his family. With young children, it is often very difficult to balance his commitments to his congregation and those at home. Rabbi Schwartz believes you have to prioritize your life and sometimes he says, "It can be very difficult."

I asked Rabbi Schwartz about his conception of God. He answered saying, "God is very complicated. My sense of God is that He is a presence and a power or force. God," he says, "is very difficult to understand and come to terms with…a lot of the relationship with God has to do with the sort of struggling and wrestling [for meaning]. That is my major model for understanding…engaging in a relationship with God, [that says] that God is necessary in our lives because we need to understand that there is something more [to life] than human beings. If we start thinking that human beings are it, then I believe that is very dangerous. God represents in some ways the mystery of the universe i.e., something we can't fully understand; that God can be both immanent and transcendent simultaneously, which is one of the mysteries of God…that we can have an experience of God being so distant – so far away, that we think God isn't there and then, in the next moment, we can have a very immediate experience of God and I think that it's different for every person. I think that the religious experience…the sense of Holiness and the feeling of God, is one that is one of the most personal experiences that one can have. It is almost impossible for me to describe it…you can never know what I feel and I can never feel what you feel."

I asked the Rabbi if he believed that God was just our Creator or was our personal God as well. He answered me saying, "yes and no." He referred to one of the statements of one of the most influential Jewish philosophers and scholars of the Talmud, Moses Maimonidies, who said, "God set the world in motion and the world goes according to the way it goes."

"I don't see God as reaching into the world on a day to day basis to cure sick people or to stop something terrible from happening," says Rabbi Schwartz. "On the other hand, I think the experience of

God can be something very personal from the human experience. Some people say 'can God hear me when I pray.' I don't think that is the question. I think God is incorporeal; the question is what does the act of prayer do to us? Does it help us feel that we have had an experience with God and then does that help us to live our lives in a better way? A *Midrash* talks about the purpose of *mitzvot*. For example," Rabbi Schwartz says, "does it make a difference if you put on *tefillin* in the morning? Do you think God cares about that? The question is what does it do for you? The *Midrash* says that the *mitzvot* are given to us to refine us, to make us more noble people, better people, more soulful people, and I think that within the structure of the *mitzvot*, that really works, and also living through the structure of the *mitzvot* gives you a sense of structure in your life."

I asked the Rabbi about his concept of the soul. Rabbi Schwartz said, "I think the soul is a very important idea and something that I believe in very much. I believe that there is more than our physical body and that it is a piece of us that continues to exist after our physical bodies are no longer functioning, and in some ways I understand that the body is sort of a vessel that holds the soul while the soul is in this world. A famous *Midrash* says that the first thing and last thing in life is the same…it is the breath. When a baby is born, they inhale and when we die, we exhale. When the baby inhales, God is putting the soul into the body and when a person dies, He is taking the soul back. That is a beautiful *Midrash*. I love the prayer in the beginning of our prayer book. It starts '*Elohai n'shama shenatata.*' The soul that God has given us is pure. It goes on – You have created it, You have formed it, You breathed it into me. And I love that idea that the soul is really the pure piece of us – maybe the piece of us that is closest to God; that has the most connection to God and that based on the way we live our lives and the choices we make and things that happen to us and some of the things we don't choose e.g., where we are born, who our parents are – that has a lot to do with what our souls end up being, as it goes through the course events of life. One renowned Talmudic scholar said we should strive to achieve a soul that is always leaping towards Heaven."

"What about Heaven?" I asked the Rabbi. "Do you believe it exists?" The Rabbi answered me: "Heaven is an amorphous concept in Judaism. *Olam Ha-ba* – the world to come - is a messianic time when the world to come will be brought into this world, when Jews will be resurrected and brought back to *Eretz Yisroel* (Land of Israel.) Then there is the question of what happens between now and then. The best explanation is the idea that the soul is in God's presence. When someone dies, their physical body cannot interact with the world anymore, but their spiritual sense continues to interact with the world. It just does," he says. "It's undeniable. Some people say that this is memory; in a way it is memory, but in some ways it's more than memory."

Rabbi Schwartz comments on free will and choices. He says that he doesn't believe in the idea of predestiny. Rather, he believes in the concept of free will i.e., that we have choices in our lives. He says, "there is a certain amount of randomness in the world. We don't have ultimate control, but that doesn't necessarily mean that God has a plan for us." I followed up my questioning with "what about being inscribed in the book of life – how does that fit into the equation?" Rabbi Schwartz replied that he believes in that concept symbolically and metaphorically. When I pressed him further about my impressions that there seems to be more deaths around the High Holy Days, he responded affirmatively. He indicated that, ironically, there do seem to be more funerals both before and after Rosh Hashanah, Yom Kippur and Pesach as well.

I asked Rabbi Schwartz what was the hardest thing he had to do as a Rabbi. He said, "the hardest thing I had to do was to be with a family whose baby was dying. It was devastating for the family and me. When you have a tragic loss [like this], the best you can do is to let them know you are there with them, give them a hug, hold their hand."

I asked the Rabbi if he had ever lost his faith in God. He replied, "no" but said, "I have struggles with God…that He is so distant and unapproachable; it [the struggle] goes back and forth."

"How do you handle all of the difficult questions that are posed to you?" I asked. "Do you answer every question put to you?" " I don't feel like I have to answer all questions posed to me," he replied. "Just because I am a Rabbi," he pauses and smiles, [doesn't mean I have all of the answers]. "If I don't know the answer, I tell them I don't know."

In questioning the Rabbi, I asked him about his feelings concerning miracles and whether he ever witnessed one. Rabbi Schwartz said, "I would say that I believe in daily miracles. In the *Amidah* prayer, we thank God for the miracles that happen every day.

You can see God's presence in the birth of a baby, to stand at the edge of the Grand Canyon, or to look at your hand and…the way the hand works is a miracle. I was watching a tree the other day and noticed the white petals falling off and there were leaves forming underneath the blossoms. I see miracles in the world and not miracles coming from outside the world."

Chapter Twenty-five
Cantor Thom King

Cantor Thom King was born in Westerly, Rhode Island, but was raised in Willington, Connecticut, a rural area located not far from the University of Connecticut. Cantor King is one of nine children. He has four living sisters and three brothers. He is married to Shazy, nee Hopfenberg, and has three lovely daughters who are the apples of his eye.

The Cantor studied voice at the Hartt School of Music at the University of Hartford where he received his degree in Music. Cantor Arthur Koret, the so-called "Cantor of Cantors," who was also responsible for the Cantor's first exposure to Judaism, was his teacher and mentor. Besides teaching at the University and leading services for 38 years at Emanuel Synagogue in Hartford, Cantor Koret became a national figure in Jewish Liturgical Music. He also served as president of the Cantor's Assembly of America.

While attending the Hartt School, Cantor King met his wife, Shazy, who was also a music student at the Conservatory. Because of the confluence of his bride-to-be, who was Jewish, and that of his teacher and mentor, Cantor Koret, Cantor King considered converting to Judaism. He went through a nominal conversion and, afterwards, a Reform Rabbi married the couple. Cantor King's ambition in school was to sing opera and he did exactly that. He has performed in opera companies across the country and continues to perform locally. Two of the most prestigious engagements for the talented baritone were his soloist performance of Mozart's *Requiem* at Carnegie Hall as well as his solo performance at the Alice Tully Hall at the Lincoln Center in New York City. He toured the country with various opera companies including the Miami, Chautauqua, and Texas Opera Theatres.

Ten years into their marriage, Thom decided he was interested in becoming a Cantor. After consulting with his teacher and mentor, Arthur Koret, and the advice of the esteemed Rabbi Haskel Lindenthal of Bloomfield, Connecticut, he went through an Orthodox conversion and the couple was remarried in an Orthodox ceremony.

Cantor King began chanting services in the *shul* where he underwent his conversion. He confided that learning Hebrew was difficult, but he mastered it in short order. He said, "I am pretty good with languages. The more I did it, the easier it became." He went on to say that everything he learned about being a Cantor came from his teacher, self-study and practical experience. The Cantor holds a commission from the Cantor's Assembly, which was acquired after he met the appropriate work and test requirements.

Cantor King was working at Emanuel Synagogue in Hartford, Connecticut, when he applied to Beth El in 1997. With his contract at Emanual about to expire, the zealous Cantor confides that he had to fill big shoes at Beth El Congregation. Cantor Hammerman previously announced his retirement and the congregation was searching for a replacement. That someone had to be one with some vocal stature to fill the emotional and physical void left by the esteemed Chazan.

"I remember meeting Rabbi Loeb and our organist, Bruce Eicher," the Cantor recalls. "We hit it off, right from the beginning," he says. "The first time I led the service, I enjoyed it a lot." When I asked the Cantor about some of his innovations in the services since coming to Beth El, he replied, "I am an evolutionist in my thinking, I believe in innovation, but not at the cost of tradition. You have to respect the history of Beth El. There are some elements that you never want to change because they are ingrained within the tradition." He cites some of the melodies as an example. "Some refer to it as *Mi-Sinai* melodies, supposedly coming from Mt. Sinai."

"There are some that want everything to be different and then there are others who don't want anything to change. Trying to maintain the balance is the most difficult part of my job." Cantor King says that he has tried to modernize some of the services, but is careful not to go overboard.

Peter G. Engelman

I asked Cantor King about the bongos and tambourines he frequently plays as part of the Friday night services. I asked him if he didn't think he was going overboard by introducing such non-traditional instruments to the service and whether those who were saying *Kaddish* might be offended by it. The good-natured Cantor smiled when he answered me. "The key to the Friday evening and *Shabbat* service is to provide a joyous uplifting service. We are very sensitive to the fact that there may be mourners attending those services, but the spirit of *Shabbat* takes precedence over the spirit of mourning. I know it might be difficult for a mourner to be thrust into such a happy situation, but they need to understand that our tradition is founded around *Shabbat*." He went on to say that he would hope that, in some circumstances it would actually help those in mourning to get a spiritual uplift.

Cantor King enjoys leading the congregation from the pulpit. He refers to being the *Sheliach Tzibbur*, the emissary of the congregation or representative before God. He points out that, unlike other religions where the spiritual leader performs prayer on behalf of others, Judaism requires that individuals pray for themselves. He says, "anyone can be a *Ba'al Tefilah* (leader of prayers) in Judaism."

Cantor King believes that his job is to touch the congregation emotionally or viscerally, to help create the atmosphere for prayer, so that the congregation can connect with God. The Cantor says that he has never been much of a believer in a personal God because, he says, "then God can change depending on the individual. My view," he says, "is that God is the Creator of the universe; that he is vitally interested in what happens to people, but who allows people to make their own mistakes [and decisions]." He goes on to say that he believes God is omniscient; that He sees everything and knows of your choices before you even make them.

Speaking about prayer, the Cantor refers to the numerous requests we make of God in our daily services. He says we expect Him to respond to our prayers and we hope that He hears our prayers but, more importantly, we need to form the bond between Him and ourselves and, through that bond, we can become spiritually strengthened. Concerning praying for someone who is ill, the Cantor prays with fervor and conviction that God will heal those who are ill, but he also says, "realistically we don't know if He will answer favorably." He quotes an old adage: "God answers all prayers, except sometimes the answer is no."

I asked him about his concepts of the soul. He quotes the same passage in our morning prayer book as Rabbi Schwartz: "The soul that You gave to me is pure; You gave it to me when I was born; You take it back when I am gone."

We concluded our interview with my question about miracles. Cantor King referred me to our daily prayer book that thanks God for all of the daily miracles He bestows upon us. "Anything that makes you understand how precious life is and how wonderful it is, is a miracle."

As I went to turn off my recorder, I noticed the computer on Cantor King's credenza. It reminded me of another question to ask. With all of the scientific breakthroughs and the advances in medical and biological research, I asked the Cantor if he thought we would ever come closer to understanding the concept of God. Cantor King answered my hypothetical question saying, "God exists on a totally different plane. Normally science is used to disprove the existence of God and sometimes dismisses much of it as superstition. I don't think that computers or science bring us any closer to [understanding] God; in fact I think they distract us from the true search for God within ourselves."

Chapter Twenty-six
Rabbi Mark G. Loeb

Rabbi Mark G. Loeb was born and raised in Boston, Massachusetts. He is the youngest of three children. He has two older sisters. The Rabbi's mother came from a traditional Jewish family where her father and brothers were all kosher butchers. Rabbi Loeb's father was not nearly as *frum* (observant) as his mother, so he was raised more Conservative than Orthodox. The Rabbi attended Hebrew School -Talmud Torah as a child, attending four afternoons a week as well as every Sunday morning. The Rabbi was Bar Mitzvahed at Temple B'nai Moshe in Boston. He completed High School in Orlando, Florida when his family moved to the sunny south.

After high school, Rabbi Loeb attended Reed College in Portland, Oregon, where he studied history, English literature and music. After college, he returned to Orlando where he was recruited by a local Rabbi to assist in the congregation's afternoon Hebrew school. Two years later, he considered the Rabbinate for the first time, believing that the experience would be intellectually stimulating. Furthermore, he thought that he might pursue a course in academia while having a foot in an active community. After three years at the Jewish Theological Seminary in New York, the Rabbi took a three-year hiatus from his studies to pursue his cultural interests in the arts. During that period, he did a lot of traveling, attended operas and museums and made many good friends. He supported himself by working for the United

Synagogue of Conservative Judaism in New York, the national association of Conservative synagogues, founded in 1913.

He decided to complete his Rabbinate studies at the Hebrew Union College in New York because of its reputation as an institute of intellectual studies. In his last year at the College, Rabbi Loeb served as a Pulpit Rabbi at a synagogue in New Jersey. Every weekend, he would commute back and forth from his New York apartment.

After he graduated, he continued his affiliation with the New Jersey congregation and enjoyed serving its congregation. It was a young congregation with a lot of growth potential. In 1975, Rabbi Loeb met Rabbi Agus, of blessed memory, for the first time. At the time, Beth El was looking for an Assistant Rabbi and Rabbi Loeb applied for the job. Although he was offered the position, Rabbi Loeb declined the offer because of his current affiliation and other personal reasons. A year later, Rabbi Loeb found out that the position in Baltimore was still open. He contacted Rabbi Agus again and, after an interview and some negotiations, accepted the position with Beth El.

Rabbi Loeb officiated at Beth El for the first time on January 2, 1976. It was a Friday evening service and the Rabbi recalls his sermon. "I gave a sermon about the then new epidemic of divorce." He said that the sermon was well received and that the congregation greeted him warmly. At first, he considered his pulpit with Beth El as tentative and thought that after a few years he might move on. As time passed, the Rabbi became more endeared to the congregation and decided to make it his home. When Rabbi Agus, of blessed memory, retired in 1980 after serving Beth El for thirty years, Rabbi Loeb assumed his senior position with the congregation. Rabbi Agus continued to serve as Rabbi Emeritus until his death in 1986. Rabbi Loeb says of Rabbi Agus: "He was a mentor and then some; we were wonderful colleagues and we were good friends. He was extraordinary as an intellectual and a human being."

Rabbi Loeb, known for his talents as an orator, delivers most of his sermons with only notes or key phrases. In delivering his speeches, the Rabbi says he organizes his thoughts first and the words follow. He goes on saying, "If you want to build an argument, you can't leave out a part of it and then [have it] make sense to yourself as you are speaking." In high school, the Rabbi participated in the debating society and took part in the acting program. I asked him if officiating at the pulpit was like acting on the stage. He replied, "that in a way it is, but that on the pulpit you are freer than on the stage, because on the pulpit you can write your own script."

Aside from his skills as an orator, Rabbi Loeb is very well known for his activism in the Jewish community. He is a board member of The Institute for Christian and Jewish Studies, The Baltimore Hebrew University, Mazon, and a host of other Jewish organizations.

I asked Rabbi Loeb what was the most difficult part of his job at Beth El. He replied saying, "I find that the hardest part of serving in the Pulpit Rabbinate is that the incessant demands of the position rob you of the kind of quiet sustained time that is needed to read without distraction, which is the basic requirement for serious reflection. A Rabbi in a pulpit is busy 24/7 and cannot stand back from the constant pressures of the job, which is discouraging." I followed up: "What are the most pleasant aspects of the Rabbinate?" "I enjoy the interplay with people, especially in areas of deep personal connection. It feels like a special privilege to share such moments in many of which I get to bring something meaningful to the lives of others."

I asked Rabbi Loeb to give me his understanding of God and the way that He affects our lives as Jews. Rabbi Loeb replied saying, "God is an idea, as Morechai Kaplan said, 'an idea that is part of the civilization of the Jewish people.' I don't have any sense that the reality of God is so important that people should fight over it. The idea of God is one that is far more overpowering than we can even begin to achieve in describing it because it's like looking at the sun – you can't! It's too much. It is not reducible in human terms of speech to describe what God is.

The mystery of the universe is what Paul Tillich [1886-1965], the noted Protestant thinker, called the 'ultimate concern' or the 'dimension of ultimate concern;' it's what Heschel said, 'fear and trembling in the presence of that which is unknowable.' Martin Buber said, 'whatever God is we don't know but we know that in the history of humankind, there have been encounters with the unknown.' We know that different people, different cultures, had moments of revelation and, we think we had one too at Sinai in the context of being freed from slavery – given the opportunity to lead free lives - and, there are those who thought, Moses among them, that he heard or intuited the presence of God as a Commanding God, who wanted our people to live a commanded life…and I find that less than fully spiritual. As Rosenzweig said, 'God is far more than the words of the

Torah.' The words were the response to the inspiration and it was as if the inspiration was powerfully felt, but not articulated. The articulator, in our case Moses, was the person who responded to the way he felt. In that sense, it is a human document and our sense of God is...[that] we assume spiritual reality is behind it all and that spiritual reality is unknowable. All that we can do, is stand in awe of it and to realize that we are not anything comparable to it, whatever it is, in its presence, our feelings about it – about nature – about the universe, we are very little dots in an ocean of reality. If you see it in the dimension of *ultimate concern*...it's the challenge for us to respond to it as Moses did to it. If we see pain, we respond with compassion; if we see tragedy, we respond with comfort. Those things matter to me...far more than our relationship to God is our relationship to each other, which should reflect what our relationship to God ought to be."

Rabbi Loeb offered his opinion on the writing of the Torah. He said, "the Jewish people wrote the Torah, perhaps inspired by God or [inspired by God] through Moses. I say that our ancestors may have understood it as a Commanding God for various reasons and, as a Commanding God, we do listen with special ears, but on the other hand, we give tradition a definite vote in what we do...but as was said by a great teacher, 'it's a vote and not a veto,' because some of what it says needs to be interpreted anew and when we fail to do that, it doesn't deserve to evolve."

The Rabbi says he still believes that the Bible is a source of great wisdom and we need to pay attention to what it says. As far as prayer, it is part of the discipline of life and there is something in it that one has to relate to, even when you don't feel like it, because it's sort of like medicine. "You take it every day. You may or may not understand how it works, but the doctor says take this pill and you will feel better. I think prayer has the dynamic where, if you engage in it, it does certain things that are very important for the human personality. So when people pray, they are stopping the clock and checking up on their soul."

"What about the soul?" I asked the Rabbi. "What is your concept of it?" "The soul is whatever it is that sustains life for us as long as we are alive. It gives us consciousness."

The Rabbi continues his thought about prayer. "When people are praying, they are giving to themselves a spiritual examination. That is at least what we do when we come to synagogue. When we are doing that, we are engaging ourselves in something very useful and important and that is that one is trying to remember before you go out and start the day, what are the things that are important to you, so you just don't get up and start winging it at life – you need to have a moment to think about some of the more important issues of life, which is why you got out of bed.

You also need to realize that there is a community of others and that part of life is not just getting out of bed and doing one's own thing all of the time. When you go to a *minyan*, you are making it possible for others to say *Kaddish* – you are identifying yourself as a part of a Jewish group that has a philosophy of life that we have been sustaining for thousands of years. There's a sense of connectiveness to Godliness and concerns of that kind, so there's also a part of us that Heschel refers to that [says] 'it is abnormal for us not to pray.' It is a way of looking at the world and saying 'My God,' I may have my daily *tzoris* (problems) but you know what? It's an 'incredible world.' There are always miracles around that we need to pause and recognize – no matter how good or bad we feel, and prayer orients us back to that kind of world. You are thinking thoughts that are more elevated other than things like 'what am I going to cook for dinner.' The idea of prayer is therapeutic and elevating, etc."

The Rabbi talks about praying for something that you really need rather than praying for something that you want. He says that when we pray for someone who is ill, we should pray not only for the person who is ill, but for our own inspiration and strength so as to make us better able to cope with a situation which is beyond the scope of our control. We should focus on how lucky we are that these people matter to us, that we are not without hope, or without family or friends. He says that prayer is not just about what you can get out of God.

Summing up the Rabbi says, "I am from the school of rational thinking [and] I don't believe in wasting time speculating about things that I have no way of validating."

Chapter Twenty-seven
Saul Z. Hammerman, Cantor Emeritus

Cantor Saul Z. Hammerman was born the youngest of six children. Of his two brothers and three sisters, only one sister is still living. The Cantor was raised in an Orthodox home in Brooklyn, New York. His parents, of blessed memory, were of modest means, but what they lacked in wealth was made up by love. The Cantor jokes about his father who, because he was so musical, would only use a "Singer" sewing machine. His grandparents were Chasidic Jews and he was very close with both of them. The Cantor showed me a picture of his grandparents, of blessed memory, which he displays prominently in his second floor private study. He remembers going on long walks to s*hul* with his grandfather, and listening to the many stories that this white bearded Chasid shared with him. He prides himself on being half Chasid as he reflects on his Jewish values and beliefs.

Cantor Hammerman shared with me the fact that, at eight years old, he was already singing in synagogue choirs and performing in Yiddish shows. As a youngster, he recalls coming home from s*hul*, putting on a tall *yarmulke* and standing in front of a mirror pretending to be a Cantor.

His ambition was fulfilled years later during his two and half year service in the Navy, where he assisted the chaplain in leading services throughout the Hawaiian Islands. After his term of service, the Cantor came back to Brooklyn and attended private Cantorial classes with his older brother. His first performance as a Cantor was in Bensonhurst in

Brooklyn, where he was hired as Chazan for the Pesach services. While completing his studies, he worked for a synagogue in Passaic, New Jersey, where he led the weekend services. He continued in that capacity for two years. Besides his private Cantorial studies, Cantor Hammerman also had private voice lessons and attended the American Theatre Wing, where he took classes in music and voice technique.

With his gifted tenor voice, the Cantor thought about going into musical comedy and, in fact, auditioned for one of Jerome Kern's productions, *Music in the Air, a Revival*. Out of hundreds of tenor applicants, he was chosen as one of the five finalists for the ensemble. Because the opening night's performance was scheduled on the first night of Rosh Hashanah and because the Cantor was previously booked to officiate, he turned down the opportunity, a decision he has never regretted.

While officiating in New Jersey, Cantor Hammerman also conducted a weekly radio show every Sunday at station "WEVD" in New York. On the show, he sang Jewish music.

In early 1952, he was interviewed by Rabbi Jacob Agus, of blessed memory, together with a committee from Beth El, who interviewed him at the Seminary in New York. At the time of his interview, he was 26 years old. The Cantor remembers being quizzed by all of these prominent businessmen and compared himself to General Custer at Little BigHorn, where the Indians surrounded him. They asked him to audition in Baltimore for a *Shabbat* service. He came to Baltimore and stayed with Boris Katz, a renowned businessman and Zionist in the Baltimore community. He officiated on that *Shabbat* and, the next day, he was offered the job as Cantor of Beth El. At the time, there were only about 350 families in the congregation. After the Cantor came to Baltimore, he took courses at the Peabody Institute to enhance his Cantorial abilities.

I asked the Cantor about his views on the obligations of a Cantor towards his congregation. The Cantor says, "I believe the responsibility of a Cantor is to infuse spirituality into the worshippers i.e., to elevate the service to where one can say, I was in *shul*." He says that he is the *Shliach Tzibor*, the emissary of his flock. "When he [the Cantor] walks down [the aisle] with *Hinini* [literally meaning - here I am], the [Rosh Hashanah] prayer that opens up the season…that all of a sudden there is an opening somewhere to hear the plea of the Chazan, praying for his flock - praying for forgiveness." Many Cantors regard *Hinini*, The

Chazan's Prayer, as the most important prayer for them, because of its powerful and humbling content. Read the words of the first part of the prayer to understand the significance of this moving liturgy.

'Here I stand, deficient in good deeds,
Overcome by awe, and trembling
In the presence of Him who abides
Amid the praises of Israel

I have come to plead with You
On behalf of Your people Israel who have sent me,
Though I am unworthy for this sacred task.

God of Abraham, God of Isaac and God of Jacob,
Gracious and merciful God, God of Israel,
Awesome and majestic God
I beseech You to help me
As I seek mercy for myself
And for those who have sent me.'

After being engaged by the congregation, the Cantor was requested to perform at several concerts and required the services of an accompanist. He called the Peabody and asked if they had a Jewish student who might be available. You guessed it! The Peabody sent out Aileen Goldstein, who eventually became Mrs. Saul Hammerman. The Hammermans have three children from their union, all of whom are married. Saul and Aileen now have six beautiful grandchildren. The couple will celebrate their 49th wedding anniversary this year.

I asked the Cantor how he feels when he chants the various prayers from the *bimah,* particularly whether he felt like a performer or one in communication with the Almighty "That's a very interesting question," he replied. "Normally I am trying to communicate with God. If, God forbid however, you have a frog in your throat," he continued, smiling, "I guarantee you that you are not thinking about communicating with God – you are thinking about that frog in your throat and vocally how to shift gears so that you don't mess up [the prayer]. A prayer has to convey meaning. I can't sing the same prayer the same way every week. It's not within me. I have to change weekly…it becomes a sameness and that's not me. Improvisation is a very important component of Chazanut (The theory and practice of synagogical liturgy.) In order for me to swim in this ocean of prayer I have to change [my melodies]." The Cantor explains that the first order of business is to inspire yourself on the *bimah* and to convey that inspiration to your congregation. He also believes that the structure of the service is paramount. He recalls going to s*hul* as a child and knowing which holiday it was just by hearing the intonations of the prayers being chanted by the Chazan.

The Cantor goes on to talk about his concept of God. He says, "I like to think of God as a big brother. I feel you need God when you don't need God and when you do need God. He is someone that you can communicate with. If I didn't believe that I was communicating with God, I couldn't be a Chazan. It would sound wooden to me." To add emphasis he says, "If you don't feel when you are in *shul* like you are in *shul*, then you are not in *shul*." He talks about how you don't have to be in *shul* to feel like you are in *shul*, citing a moment in an elevator where suddenly a spiritual thought might come to him.

I asked Cantor Hammerman about his belief in *beshert*. "I am half Chasid," the Cantor answered, "and I believe in *beshert*, but [I also believe that] you have to help God [to help yourself]."

As far as our prayer books and Torah, Cantor Hammerman believes that the words were written by man, but inspired by God. He compares the inspiration of Moses with that of Brahms, Einstein and Mozart.

He says that the hardest part of being a Cantor is the sadness that he has personally experienced from losses within the congregation. His most joyous times are when he and his family attend services together. As far as personal mentors, he mentions his father-in-law, Pete Goldstein, of blessed memory, with whom he was very close. Professionally, he mentions his teachers and other Cantors such as Israel Alter, the chief Cantor of Johannesburg, South Africa, and Pierre Pinchik, one of the greatest Cantors of our time who, he jokingly says, could make water come from a stone.

During his 51 years with Beth El, Cantor Hammerman brought and introduced to Baltimore many famous musicians and singers. He mentions Rene Fleming, the world-renowned soprano opera star, Itzhak Perlman, Schlomo Mintz and Gil Shaham, all noted violinists.

He refers to himself as the Sol Hurok of Baltimore. He talks about having a great career and being blessed. He says, "I love being Cantor Emeritus. I like doing things on my time. I am still involved in getting projects off the ground as always." He mentions his current project of organizing the retired Cantors around the country. They are planning their second gathering at the Saxony Hotel in Miami Beach.

Cantor Hammerman earned an honorary doctorate degree from the Jewish Theological Seminary; is past president of The Cantor's Assembly, and the recipient of their 2003 Kavod award. He is also the founder of the Cantor's Association of Baltimore and has recorded four albums of Jewish content. Saul and his lovely wife, Aileen, have performed together on many stages throughout the world and both have enjoyed distinguished careers. Saul considers himself to be truly blessed. He seems to be very much at ease with his position as Cantor Emeritus and is busily enjoying his retirement.

Chapter Twenty-eight
Conclusions

After interviewing 19 "Minyanaires," my granddaughter, Jillian Shure, Ritual Director, Sandy Winters, Cantor Thom King, Rabbi Steve Schwartz, Rabbi Mark Loeb and Saul Hammerman, Cantor Emeritus, I must admit, I have learned a great deal; not only of their individual beliefs and convictions, but more about my own. The diversity of religious backgrounds among the "Minyanaires" is significant yet, for many, their religious beliefs have converged into similar practice within the synagogue.

There are those who came from very Orthodox families, where literal interpretations of the Torah and Talmud were taught, and where God is portrayed as an active, personal God who, when petitioned, grants favors to those who are righteous and punishes those who do not adhere strictly to His laws. This interpretation of God is referred to in philosophical circles as the Commanding God - One who is to be feared and revered. Today, many Conservative and Reform Jews lean towards a more liberal understanding of God: one where He is considered more transcendent than immanent, more passive than active, more forgiving than punishing. Many of these same people remain convinced that God is unknowable and that prayer is more for self-examination and necessary for spiritual bonding with that unknowable presence.

The more traditional worshippers believe in the daily interactivity of God, including His dynamic role in petitionary and intercessional prayer. Despite the diversity and dimensions of belief that exist within the group of "Minyanaires," none of their individual positions appears to affect their attendance, participation, or camaraderie. All seemingly pray with the same fervor, bowing, swaying and singing in harmony with each other and with whomever their leaders in prayer happen to be on any given day. In my opinion, the most beautiful part of the *Shacharit*, *Mincha* or *Maariv* service is not the recitation of any single prayer or psalm, but rather the performance of the *minyan* as a group, interacting in a way that heightens the spiritual bonding of all with one another.

***

The argument over whether God is either an active, personal God or an inactive, passive God or a combination of both, has gone on since the time of Abraham. Cicero (106-43 BCE), the famous Roman orator, lawyer, politician and philosopher, thought the subject was so important that he asked the world to consider the various doctrines and determine which was true.

Maimonidies/Rambam, Rabbinic authority, codifier, philosopher, and royal physician (1134 –1204 CE), tried to tackle the subject when he formulated his *Guide of the Perplexed* where he held in *Book V*, Chapters 17-19, that as regards human beings, providence does indeed operate at the level of the individual. It is only as regards species, which are not bearers of the *Tzelem Elohim* (Divine Image), that providence is said to operate somewhat generically. And as other passages in the Guide make clear, Maimonides held that it is precisely because human beings are made in the Divine Image that providence, for us, operates at the individual level. For Maimonides, that image consists of the power of reason and intellect and one of the most important ways in which providence operates in the world is through the active exercise of human intelligence.

Sandy Winters, Beth El's Ritual Director, who regularly reads the Torah portions during the morning *minyan* and teaches Torah classes, does not believe that God is active in terms of His powers of intercession. She says, "I recite the prayers because there is an esthetic value; the origin of the Hebrew word, *tefillah*, (prayer) is self examination; that to me is what prayer is [all about]. It pulls me into a structural thing because it's something that I wouldn't do otherwise."

Cantor King believes that God is the Creator of our universe and that He is vitally interested in what happens to people, but allows them to make their own decisions and mistakes. He also believes that God is omniscient in that He sees everything and knows beforehand of the choices we will make. As far as prayer, he says that he hopes God hears our prayers, but that it is more important that we form a bond with Him so that we can become spiritually strengthened.

Rabbi Schwartz talks about his wrestling with the many questions that arise when talking about God's activity in our daily lives. "I have struggles with God that He is so distant and unapproachable; [the struggle] it goes back and forth." He says, "God represents in some ways the mystery of the universe i.e., something that we can't fully understand – that God can be both immanent and transcendent simultaneously." He talks about how we can have an experience that is very distant and then, in the next moment, we can have one that is immediate and personal.

Rabbi Loeb, a scholar from the school of rational thinking, says, "I don't believe in wasting time speculating about things that I have no way of validating." He is more concerned with man's relationship with man. The Rabbi believes that the spirit of Godliness is how we respond to the needs of others. He believes that God may have inspired Moses and our people, but that He is unknowable and is thereby part of the *ultimate concern* of all humanity.

Cantor Hammerman believes that he couldn't be a Chazan if he didn't believe that he could communicate with God. He looks at God as a big brother – someone whom you can talk to when you need Him and when you don't need Him.

One can see from all of the discussion that the questions and answers about our Almighty God are varied and diverse. It is indeed difficult to arrive at any verifiable conclusions in the field of theology. Philosophers and learned men of all ages have attempted to set forth their own axioms, postulates or universal truths about the existence of God and our creation, only to return to the drawing board again and again. There is only one thing certain when it comes to the unknowable and that is: the unknowable is unknowable.

On the other hand, one does not necessarily have to have proof for everything to prove that it exists. We see a door and know that a carpenter created it. We don't know who the carpenter is, but we know that he exists or existed. We cannot empirically prove a carpenter created the door but do we deny that he created it? We don't because, based on our intellect and reasoning and our faith that our senses are accurate barometers of essential truths, we acknowledge that, even without proof, a carpenter created the door.

So the same can be said about the infinite and miraculous creations that abound about us. We may not ever be able to prove conclusively that God has created these wonders but, as with the carpenter, we reason that none of this marvel and beauty would have ever been possible without the existence of our Creator. Again, we trust our intuitions and senses and refer to it as faith.

This book is about those who have faith — some feel it stronger than others do because it has been engrained in them from their childhood. It is as natural to them as eating a meal. On the other hand, there are those who feel it because of deliberation and deductive reasoning. One might refer to them as the intellectuals i.e., those who have studied and given much thought to the whole idea of the existence of God before accepting Him. Finally there are those who believe because they need to believe. They innately understand that we are not unto ourselves — that we need the help of someone who is much greater than us to help us along life's paths.

Faith is the bottom line in religious practice. The manner in which it is acquired or achieved appears to be of little consequence. Rabbi Jacob Agus, of blessed memory, put it very well.

> Man alone is capable of thinking of himself as an individual, set over against the universe. As we grow day by day in self-consciousness and self-understanding, we become more deeply aware both of our loneliness and relatedness to the overarching all-inclusive Almighty God. As we strive for personal fulfillment, we realize ever more keenly the inexorable boundaries of our existence and infinite power and vastness of the Life of the Universe, which throbs but for a brief moment in our veins. Thus, as we seek our own deepest self, we come to find it ultimately in God. As Hillel put it, 'If I am not for myself, who will be for me? — But if I am only for myself, what am I?'
>
> Selah

Publisher's Note

In order to honor the daily mitzvot of the "Minyanaires," around the world, Terumah Publishing will donate 10% of the profits from the sale of this book to the Prayer Book Fund of the Beth El Congregation of Baltimore, Maryland. That portion of the purchase price may be deductible for Income Tax purposes as a charitable contribution under Section 170 (c) of the Internal Revenue Code. Please check with your financial advisor as to the amount of your deduction.

Religious organizations wishing to purchase quantities of this book may consult with the publisher as to special pricing.

Terumah Publishing
Baltimore, Maryland